HISTORIC SCOTLAND

SCOTLAND'S HISTORIC SHIPWRECKS

COLIN MARTIN

B. T. Batsford Ltd / Historic Scotland

Typeset by Bernard Cavender Design & Greenwood Graphics Publishing
and printed by The Bath Press, Bath

Published by B. T. Batsford Ltd
583 Fulham Road, London SW6 5BY

A CIP catalogue record for this book is
available from the British Library.

ISBN 0 7134 8327 6 (limp)
ISBN 0 7134 8328 8 (cased)

(Front cover) A diving archaeologist from St Andrews University at
work on the wreck of the *Dartmoor* (1690) in the Sound of Mull.
(Back cover) A bronze gun is raised from the wreck of *El Gran Grifón*
(1588) off Fair Isle.

WITHDRAWN

SCOTLAND'S
HISTORIC
SHIPWRECKS

In memory of Dr David Russell

Contents

Illustrations

Colour plates

Acknowledgements

My primary debt is to all those diving archaeologists who, over the years, have worked with me underwater on many of the sites described in this book. Space precludes listing them all so I can only mention permanent members of the teams, though this in no way diminishes my indebtedness to the others. They are: Adrian Barak, Neil Dobson, Andrew Fielding, Dr Dave Gregory, Mark Lawrence, Tony Long, Paula Martin, Simon Martin, the late Keith Muckelroy, Chris Oldfield, Philip Robertson, Kevin Robinson, Sydney Wignall and Annabel Wood. Sustained non-diving support has been provided in various ways by Edward and Peter Martin and Ray Sutcliffe. In our work on the wreck off Duart Point we have been helped generously by members of the Archaeological Diving Unit (ADU), acting in both their official and private capacities; those not already mentioned include the ADU's Director, Martin Dean, and his associates Dr Antony Firth, Steve Liscoe, Jonathan Moore, Ian Oxley, Duncan Simpson and Kit Watson. Dr Ian MacLeod of the Western Australian Maritime Museum has given his time and expertise in helping us to get *in situ* conservation procedures under way. My colleagues at St Andrews University, particularly Dr Robert Prescott of the Scottish Institute of Maritime Studies, have been constant in their support.

Work on the various wrecks would not have been possible without generous donations from many organisations and individuals, including the Esmée Fairbairn Charitable Trust, the Glenfiddich Living Scotland Awards, William Grant and Sons, the Leverhulme Trust, the MacRobert Trusts, the Peter Moores Trust, the Pilgrim Trust and the Shetland Trust for Maritime Archaeology. Special acknowledgement is due to the Russell Trust which, in memory of the late Dr David Russell, helped to establish an Underwater Archaeological Field Research Unit at St Andrews.

I owe many debts to people in the museum world. The late Dr Robert Stevenson of the National Museums of Scotland (then the National Museum of Antiquities) provided encouragement, conservation support and money for the *Dartmouth* project. His successors have continued this tradition by supporting work on the *Swan*, and we must single out for special thanks Alan Saville, Theo Skinner and Dr David Caldwell. In Shetland our work would not have been possible without the local knowledge, support and boundless goodwill of the late Tom Henderson, Andrew Williamson and Tommy Watt, all of the County Museum. At St Andrews the pioneering work in supercritical drying carried out by Dr Barry Kaye and Professor David Cole-Hamilton of our Chemistry Department has opened up exciting prospects for the conservation of organic materials. The late Alison McLeay not only dived with me on the site of the Tobermorg wreck but also generously shared the fruits of her own researches into its background.

Wrecks tend to occur in remote but beautiful places, and I am grateful to many friends on Fair Isle, Barra and Mull for their support and kindness. On Mull I owe a particular debt to Sir Lachlan Maclean of Duart and his family.

The five seasons of fieldwork at Duart would not have been possible without Historic Scotland's generous financial support and sympathetic open-mindedness in what has been, for them, a new and unprecedented area of responsibility. For this particular thanks are due to Dr Noel Fojut, Richard Welander and Ron Dalziel. My editors, Dr David Breeze and Jackie Henrie of Historic Scotland, and the staff at Batsford, have been a joy to work with. Thanks also go to Paula Martin for proof reading, advice, and compiling the index.

For illustrations I am indebted to the following: The Trustees of the National Museums of Scotland (**35–6, 56, colour plates 6 and 8**), Historic Scotland (**94 and colour plate 4**, the latter being original artwork by Andrew McIlvride), The National Maritime Museum (**1, 9, 12, 16, 53**), Maritiem Museum 'Prins Hendrik', Rotterdam (**79**), The Archaeological Diving Unit (**32, 42**), Archivo General de Simancas (**4**), The Scottish Record Office (**colour plate 12**), St Andrews University Library (**10**), the *Glasgow Herald* (**14**), Ian Lowe (**2**), Edward Martin (**47, colour plate 17, and author's portrait**), Peter Martin (**57–8**), Tony Long (**66, 84, 90–1**), Jeremy Green (**colour plate 9**), and Keith Muckelroy (**68, 76–7**). The remaining illustrations are the author's.

1
'A Greate Ship of Spaigne' – the Tobermory wreck, 1588

'By mischance of gunpouder ...'

The bustling town of Tobermory on Mull is today the busiest yacht haven in the Western Isles of Scotland (**colour plate 1**). Nestled at the foot of a cliff by a spring (*Tobar Moire*, or Mary's Well) which attracted pilgrims in pre-Reformation days, its crescent-shaped waterfront protected by Calve Island provides a deep and secure natural harbour close by the north-western entrance to the Sound of Mull. But as a settlement it dates only from 1788, when it became a base for the herring fleets of the British Fisheries Company.

Two centuries before that it was a wild and almost deserted place, frequented only by the sleek war-galleys of the powerful Maclean clan who, from their base at Duart Castle at the other end of the Sound, dominated Mull and the adjacent peninsula of Morvern. Outsiders were rarely welcome, and few had cause to visit this desolate haven.

But in late September 1588 a huge ship rounded the point of Rubha na Leip and limped into the shelter of the bay (**1**). Her sails were in tatters, and she had clearly suffered from battle-damage as well as from the autumn gales, which for weeks had been blowing with unusual force. The vessel dropped anchor some 80 m (90 yds) from where the Caledonian MacBrayne pier now stands, and in due course her officers found themselves in the presence of Mull's formidable overlord, Lachlan Maclean of Duart.

In what language they conversed is not on record but the bedraggled strangers, whose leaders were resplendent in what had once been aristocratic finery, had little difficulty in communicating what they wanted. They were

1 A sixteenth-century Mediterranean great-ship (engraving after Brueghel).

2 A Spanish arquebusier of 1588. A reconstruction by Ian Lowe based on weaponry, military equipment, and clothing found on the wreck of the Armada ship *La Trinidad Valencera* off the north coast of Donegal.

local feuds. The Spanish officers agreed, and hostages were exchanged to ensure good faith. In due course 'ij cannones and a hundreth hugbotteres' from the Armada ship set forth from Mull with the Macleans to 'besege a hews of Anggues Machales'.

This was Mingary Castle, on the Ardnamurchan shore opposite Tobermory (3). The Spanish troops surrounded it but, in spite of their two pieces of artillery, the Macdonalds' ancient stronghold proved too tough a nut to crack, and after three days they called off the siege. At their new master's behest, however, they moved on to softer targets among the adjacent islands. Details of the depredations which followed survive in an arraignment for rebellion issued the following year, in which it was alleged that:

> Lauchlan McLayne of Dowart accompanyed with a grite nowmer of thevis, brokin men and sornaries of Clannis, besydis the nowmer of ane hundreth Spanyeartis, come bodin in feir of weir to his Majesteis proper ilis of Canna, Rum, Eg and the Ile of Elennole, and, aftir they had soirned, wracked and spoilled the saidis haill Illis, they treasonablie rases fyre, and in maist barbarous, shamefull and cruell maner, byrnt the same Illis, with the haill men, women and childrene being thairintill, not sparing the pupillis and infantis.

Meanwhile, back in Tobermory, repairs to the ship had been progressing for several weeks. But the presence of an Armada vessel off Mull was now widely known. To hedge his bets, Lachlan Maclean had reported her arrival to James VI in Edinburgh, and the news was transmitted to London by the English Ambassador to Scotland, William Asheby. In early November Asheby sent a second report:

> This six weeks ... [there has been] a great ship of Spaigne about the Ile of Mula in MacLanes countrie, which thei here report cannot go from thence; those irishe [i.e.

Spaniards from the great Armada which had sailed against England earlier that year, and they needed help. If they could obtain food and water they would make repairs to their ship in this sheltered anchorage, and depart in peace. Lachlan Maclean agreed to their request, but at a price.

On board the ship were several hundred troops who, though malnourished and sick from more than two continuous months at sea, were nevertheless the cream of Europe's professional soldiery (2). In return for his assistance Maclean wanted a company of them to help settle his

Gaelic Scots] people releave them with victell, but are not able to possess her, for she is well furnished both with shott and men; if there be anie shipes of war in Ireland thei might have a great praie of this ship for she is thought to be verie riche.

Two days later Asheby had further, electrifying news:

The Spannishe shipe ... is burnt, as is reported here by the treacherie of the Irishe; and almost all the men within is consumed with

3 Mingary Castle, Ardnamurchan, the Macdonald stronghold unsuccessfully besieged by Lachlan Maclean and soldiers from the *San Juan de Sicilia* in 1588.

fire; it is thought to be on[e] of the principalle shippes, and some on[e] of great accompt within; for he was alwais, as thai saie, served in sylver.

Mystery surrounds the explosion and its cause. A Spanish account derived from an inquiry held five years later blamed carelessness in spreading gunpowder on the deck to dry: while this was

13

being done 'they were engulfed by an explosion which knocked down all the men on the forward deck, and most of them died.' The ship then caught fire and sank.

The English version is rather different. In a letter written a few months after the event it was reported that 'Jhon Smollett, a man that had grett trust among the Spaniartes entred the ship and cast in the powder and a pesse of lint and so departed.' Smollett was apparently a Dumbarton merchant from whom the Spaniards were buying provisions. He may also have been an English undercover agent. On 26 November Asheby, writing to Queen Elizabeth's minister Sir Francis Walsingham, speaks enigmatically of 'the partie that laid the traine, whom we here saie to be comed into England, the man knowen to your honour and called Smallet'.

The *San Juan de Sicilia*

Controversy has long dogged the identity of the Armada ship which lies at the bottom of Tobermory Bay. In the mid seventeenth century Archbishop Spottiswoode described her as 'a ship of Florence' and this appellation has survived through the centuries under the variants *Florencia*, *Florencion* and *Florida*. A ship from the Italian port of Florence did indeed sail with the Armada. She was an up-to-date galleon belonging to the Grand Duke of Tuscany, called the *San Francisco*, and she had been requisitioned at Lisbon to take part in the campaign. Spanish sources refer to her as the *Florencia*, and it has for long been widely believed that she is the Tobermory ship.

But this identification cannot be sustained. As the Armada's meticulous records confirm, the *Florencia* returned safely to Spain. Those same records, moreover, positively identify the ship lost at Tobermory. She was the *San Juan de Sicilia*, an 800-ton argosy from the Adriatic port of Ragusa (modern Dubrovnik). Together with nine similar merchant vessels from Dalmatia and Italy she had been a member of the Armada's Levant squadron.

In civilian life the *San Juan de Sicilia* had been an Adriatic merchantman, normally engaged in shipping grain from Sicily to feed the urban population of Ragusa, although on at least one occasion she appears to have voyaged as far as England. She was originally called the *Brod Martolosi* (Martolosic̈'s Ship), after one of her owners. In 1586 she had put into a Sicilian port and was embargoed by the Spanish king's officers, Sicily being one of Philip II's dominions. Shortly afterwards 300 men of the Sicilian *Tercio* (regiment) embarked on her for Lisbon, where the Armada was assembling.

When she arrived there she was requisitioned to take part in the campaign itself, for the Armada's planners had identified a particular need for big Mediterranean-built merchant ships. Martin de Bertendona, the Levant squadron's commander, considered that their *grandeza* (a word which implies overbearing magnificence as well as sheer size) would give them an overwhelming tactical advantage when it came to close-quarter battle. His observation underlines the 'floating fortress' concept with which most Spaniards viewed naval warfare. The capital ships of the Armada were to be, in effect, mobile castles filled with troops, a Mediterranean-rooted approach to naval warfare diametrically opposite to the 'weapons platform' strategy adopted by the well-gunned and highly manoeuvrable front-line ships of Queen Elizabeth's navy.

Moreover these big Levanters had holds capable of carrying one of the Armada's most vital cargoes – the heavy siege artillery which, once on English soil, would support the planned assault on London. The *San Juan de Sicilia* was assigned two of these monsters, bronze two-and-a-half tonners which threw solid iron shot of 40 pounds. They are described in detail in the ship's manifest. The guns were cast at Augsburg by the Emperor Charles V's master-founder, Gregorio Loeffer, and bore the Imperial arms with the double-headed Hapsburg eagle. A Spanish manuscript of 1587 includes a remarkable drawing of one of these pieces (4).

Each gun was provided with two heavy field carriages (the second set was a spare) equipped

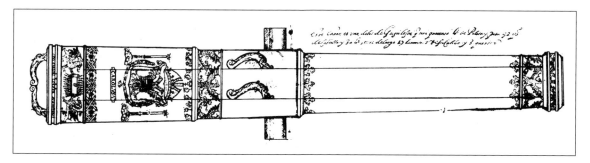

4 A bronze siege cannon by Gregorio Loeffer of Augsburg, from a manuscript of 1587 now in Simancas Castle, Spain. The Tobermory ship carried two pieces identical to this one.

with iron-bound spoked wooden wheels and articulated limbers to allow the five-ton assemblages to be drawn across country by teams of horses or oxen (5). The hold was also packed with campaign equipment: tents (to keep the ammunition dry, not the men); prefabricated timbers from which to construct gun emplacements; basketwork gabions for defensive earthworks; sharpened stakes; picks and shovels; handcarts and baskets; a massive tripod hoist for mounting and dismounting the

guns; tallow for greasing the wheel bearings, and a vast array of specialist tools and implements. There was even a field forge for the blacksmith.

Further cargo space was taken up by provisions: water and wine in cask, straw-wrapped jars of olive oil, vinegar, salt pork (only the poorer cuts were included), tuna, beans, chick-peas and hard-tack (6 and 7). This was to feed the ship's complement of 342 not only for the voyage but also during the campaign which was to follow.

5 A siege cannon from the wreck of *La Trinidad Valencera* mounted on a replica gun carriage based on components recovered during excavation.

6 An olive jar from *La Trinidad Valencera*. Height 30 cm (12 in).

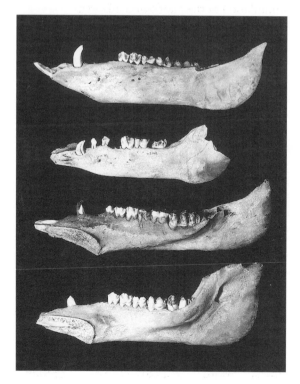

7 Butchered pig jaws from *La Trinidad Valencera*.

Of these men 279 were soldiers, assigned to the companies of Miguel de Garro Ros (*Tercio* of Sicily) and Antonio de Valcarcel (of Francisco de Toledo's *Tercio*). With them came their weapons and equipment: muzzle-loading matchlock arquebuses and muskets, 18-foot pikes of Spanish ash, morions and breastplates, and incendiary devices for close-quarter action. While at sea these men also provided crews for the ship's 26 guns, working under the direction of the master-gunners. The guns ranged in size from heavy bronze muzzle-loaders to light swivel pieces mounted on the ship's sides and upper works. To service them the ship carried 69 barrels of gunpowder, each containing one Castilian *quintal* (46 kg/100 lb). The barrels were bound with wooden hoops to minimize the danger of sparks.

In addition to the weaponry, munitions and equipment, the troops brought with them quantities of domestic and personal items. Together these objects represented many aspects of contemporary material culture, akin to the contents of a small village.

The commander of the ship was Don Diego Tellez Enriquez, son of the Commander of the Knights of Alcantara, one of Spain's foremost military orders (8). His brother, Don Pedro, sailed with him. These Spanish grandees far outranked Luka Ivanov Kinković, the *San Juan de Sicilia's* Ragusan captain.

On 14 May 1588 the Armada's 130 ships sailed from Lisbon carrying nearly 30,000 men, two-thirds of them soldiers. Their purpose was to rendezvous with 20,000 barge-borne troops under the Duke of Parma off Flanders so that, protected by the fleet, the joint invasion force could land somewhere near Margate. Once the beach-head was secured, the Armada would land a second wave of troops together with the munitions, provisions and artillery needed to launch a *blitzkrieg* assault on London.

After storms forced the fleet to put into Corunna to regroup, the Armada entered the Channel on 30 July and shook itself into a wide crescent-shaped formation. The Spaniards'

8 The gold emblem of a Knight of Alcantara, recovered from the wreck of the Armada galleass *Girona* off Antrim. It depicts the order's patron, St Julian, with his attributes of waterfall and pear tree. Length 28 mm (1in).

objective was to advance in rigid order towards the rendezvous with Parma. Within the fleet 20 or so of the most powerful and nobly-officered ships (including the *San Juan de Sicilia*) were authorized to act on their own initiatives whenever the formation as a whole was threatened. In this way a response to any English attack was guaranteed and self-regulating: no further orders would be needed to set it in train. Meanwhile the formation would continue towards its objective, leaving gaps in its ranks to which the 'troubleshooters' might return when their business was complete.

The English were at first nonplussed by the Spaniards' tight defensive formation and inexorable progress – 'we durst not adventure to put in amongst them, their fleet being so strong', wrote Lord Admiral Howard in concerned frustration. In fact the fleets were tactically stalemated. The English, whose ships were more manoeuvrable and had heavier guns, could keep clear of danger and dictate the range at which they fought, but could not physically overwhelm their adversaries. On the other hand the Spaniards were unable to engage in close combat leading to a boarding action, in which their superior military strength was likely to prevail. In strategic terms, however, the Spaniards held the advantage, for the Armada's aim was not to precipitate a decisive sea battle but to maintain unimpeded progress towards its objective.

The running fight which took place along the Channel, though not without incident, was little more than inconclusive sparring. But as Flanders drew closer the Spanish plan began to disintegrate. The shoal waters off the Flemish coast, which were dominated by aggressive shallow-draught Dutch fly-boats, had been seen by the Spanish commanders as a fatal flaw in the plan from its inception. In this narrow strip of water, where the deep-draught Armada ships could not operate, Parma's defenceless landing craft would have no protection. But the King over-ruled his subordinates' concerns, for he believed that his strategy was sanctioned and thus guaranteed by the Almighty.

In the event the divine intervention which Philip II had counted on to overcome the difficulty failed to materialize. On 7 August the Armada anchored off Calais, the last deep-water anchorage before the rendezvous. But Parma was not ready to come out: he had been given insufficient warning and, moreover, he was not prepared to expose his army to certain annihilation at the hands of the Dutch privateers. At this point the English took advantage of wind and tide, and Spanish irresolution, to send in fireships. The stratagem temporarily broke the Armada's discipline, and its ships scattered in panic towards the waiting Flemish shoals (9).

A providential shift of wind saved the Spanish fleet from the sandbanks and pushed it northwards towards deep water and it was here, off Gravelines, that the Armada revealed – albeit too late – its formidable if misapplied strength. The Spanish commander, the Duke of Medina Sidonia, placed his flagship *San Martín* between the advancing English and his own scattering fleet. Soon a number of other ships rallied to his support and formed a protective rearguard, gradually shepherding the Armada back into its defensive formation.

At this point the English threw everything into a final, desperate attack. Lord Admiral Howard's ships were almost out of ammunition, and without firepower they had no means of

9 The battle off Gravelines, following the fireship attack at Calais.

preventing the Spaniards from landing. Caution was thrown to the winds: for the first time the English galleons went in hard and close, delivering salvoes of ship-smashing broadsides. But it was not enough to break the Armada's tight mutually-supportive formation, and at last the English had to disengage because their shot-lockers were empty.

Throughout this battle the *San Juan de Sicilia* was heavily engaged. A group of English ships battered her

> so heavily with their guns that they completely shattered her ... [we had to] repair the damage from the many shots which the ship had received alow and aloft and from the prow to the stern, and below the waterline in places difficult to repair.

Another report adds that 'not a span of her sails was serviceable; and as we could not find her, it is feared she may be lost.'

Without Parma's troops the Armada plan had collapsed, and on 13 August Medina Sidonia's flagship issued orders for the return voyage home. Because the fleet was now well into the North Sea there was no alternative but the perilous north-about route around the top of Britain and into the Atlantic for the long southward run to Spain. Autumn was approaching, and the equinoctial gales of that year – the Winds of God, as their Protestant adversaries would have it – blew early and with unusual violence, and many of the returning Spanish ships were driven towards the western coasts of Scotland and Ireland. Thus it was that the crippled *San Juan de Sicilia* came to Tobermory Bay on 23 September 1588.

Her remains lie there still.

'Thirty million of money'

After the *San Juan de Sicilia's* catastrophic destruction, rumour abounded. The disaster had been precipitated by the Maclean of Duart, by treachery, witchcraft, or both. A Spanish princess had gone down with the ship. And, of course, the wreck contained a fabulous treasure, including (though this invention followed in the seventeenth century) the crown jewels which Parma was to wear as the King of Spain's viceroy in England. A late seventeenth- century report estimated the total value as 'thirty million of money', though in what currency was not specified.

The treasure legend appears to be rooted in a mysterious visit made to Spain by the 7th Earl of Argyll shortly after the wreck took place. In addition to being chief of the powerful Campbell clan, Argyll was Admiral of the Western Isles, which gave him the right to salvage shipwrecks within this area. However James VI, suspicious of Argyll's long absence in Spain, declared him a rebel, and the salvage rights reverted to the Crown.

To what extent these moves were connected with the Tobermory wreck and its supposed treasure is not clear. But in 1641 Charles I sold the rights back to the 8th Earl, who had 'heard some doukers [divers] and others expert in such matters state that they had considered it possible to recover some of the ships and their valuables'. The technology now existed whereby intrepid men could reach the ship in Tobermory Bay.

Diving bells had been known from early times (Alexander the Great is reputed to have gone down in one), but by the seventeenth century they were being used seriously to recover wrecks and their contents. Attempts were made to raise the Swedish warship *Vasa*, which sank in Stockholm Harbour during her maiden voyage in 1628, and although these were unsuccessful most of her guns were recovered in the 1660s from a depth of over 30 m (100 ft).

The bells used on the *Vasa* were truncated cones of lead sheet, a little over 1.2 m (4 ft) high, with a square platform of lead hanging under the lower rim for the diver to stand on. As some protection against the cold the divers were dressed in flexible leather suits, and carried long boat-hooks with which to grapple the wreckage and attach ropes. The bell's interior

was almost completely dark, and the water rose inside it as the pressure increased with depth. At 30 m (100 ft) it would have been level with the diver's upper chest. Work was limited to about quarter of an hour, after which the bell would have to be raised for a change of air. Skilled divers could leave the bell for brief periods to conduct work outside it, holding their breath. In the 1660s a technique for replenishing the bell by lowering barrels of air to it was introduced.

The Tobermory wreck lay in less than 20 m (66 ft) of water, well within bell-diving range. During the 1630s and '40s it appears that the Earl of Argyll managed to get diving operations under way, and a number of iron guns were recovered.

Unfortunately for the Earl (later the Marquis) of Argyll, the Civil War and its uncertain shifts of loyalty intervened. In 1653, during a Cromwellian raid on Mull, Argyll sided with the Commonwealth forces against his enemies the Macleans of Duart (see p. 47). It was a fatal move. On the restoration of monarchy in 1660 he was beheaded in the Tower for alleged complicity in Charles I's execution, and among the properties which reverted to the Crown were the rights to the Tobermory wreck. But, in the event, it turned out that Argyll had been innocent of regicide, and his confiscated estates were restored to his heir, the 9th Earl.

Within five years salvage work was underway at Tobermory. It was conducted by James Mauld, who brought with him a diving bell from Sweden. But the enterprise was dogged by problems. Argyll wrote some years later that Mauld 'wrought only three months, and most of this time was spent mending his bells and sending for materials he needed, so that he raised only two brass cannon of large calibre.' Dispirited, Mauld left for England leaving his men and equipment behind him.

Nothing daunted, Argyll continued the work on his own account, and eventually a further six bronze guns were raised. By this time other salvage entrepreneurs were coming forward. A plausible German applicant managed to recover

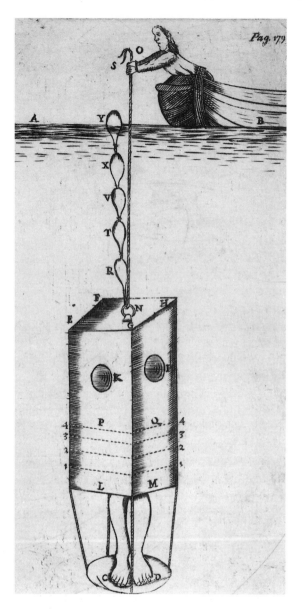

10 George Sinclair's diving 'ark', from his *Hydrostaticks* of 1672.

only an anchor before clandestinely departing, leaving considerable debts. Another was a one-time lecturer at St Andrews, George Sinclair, who went on to become Professor of Philosophy at Glasgow, where he pioneered the study of pressures in liquids and gases.

In his book *The Hydrostaticks* (1672) Sinclair sets out his design for a diving 'Ark' made of oak sealed with pitch (**10**). It was fitted with

three portholes, and in a corner the diver was advised to 'hing a little bottle with some excellent spirits, for refreshing the stomach, under Water'. Although Sinclair appears to have been involved in the 1665 operations, there is no evidence that he subsequently dived at Tobermory with his ingenious 'Ark'.

In 1677 the professionals moved in. Hans Abricht van Treilaben was the Swedish salvor who, in 1664 and 1665, had successfully recovered 53 bronze guns from the *Vasa* wreck in Stockholm harbour. No sooner had the Earl of Argyll drawn up a contract with him, however, than Charles II again intervened through his brother James, the Duke of York, to make inquiries about what was happening at Tobermory. The Duke's visit resulted in an immediate claim through the courts for the restitution of the Crown's rights to the wreck. But the claim, to James's barely-concealed fury, was not accepted. Treilaben and his partner Captain Adolpho Smith were thus free to resume their work, and a later memorandum by the 9th Earl provides an insight to these early diving operations:

[The wreck] lies in a very good road land-lok'd betwixt a litle iland and a bay in the Ile of Mull, a place quhair vessels doe ordinarily anchor, free of any violent tyde, hardly any stream at all, a clean heard channell with a litle sand on the top, and litle or no mudd in most places about, upon ten fathom at highe-water, and about eight at ground-ebb, so calm that the Earle of Argyll caused dive at all tymes of the tyde in seasonable weather, and even when it was whyt water within lesse than a mile of the place.

The report goes on to describe the condition of the wreck:

The fore part of the ship is quyt burnt, so that from the mizen mast to the fore-ship there is no deck but the hull full of sand, which the Earl of Argyll caused search a little but found nothing but a great heap of cannon-ball about the main-mast, and some ketles, and tankers of copper and such like in other places.

Over the hindship, wher the cabin was, ther is a heap of great timber, which will be a great task to remove, but under thes is the main expectation [of treasure], and it is thought the deck under the cabine is still entire. Thes great timber lay in great confusion and in the midle ther is a voyd place, which the Earle durst not try with the bell and the workmen did not give a perfect accompt of it. Thes great timber lyes so high, that ebb-water they can be touched, at five or six fathom water.

Ther is a harder and softer sand in places neir about the ship. Ther was cannon found on clean sand, quhair a six pence might be known from a shilling. Some cannon wer half covered with sand, and on[e] cannon fullie covered was gotten up, so farr does the art of the bell go.

The cannon generally lay at some yards distance from the ship from tuo to twentie and some not recovered lay crosse tuo or three together.

The hazards of diving in their bell were not the only ones Treilaben and his crew had to face. A contingent of discontented Macleans, furious that their arch-enemies the Campbells seemed to be on the brink of recovering a fortune in treasure, dug trenches nearby from which to 'shute guns, muskats, and pistols at them'.

But high politics again stepped in to deprive the Earl of Argyll of his right to seek the treasure. In 1681 the Duke of York again came to Scotland, this time to open Parliament and force through a new act enabling a Catholic (i.e. James himself) to inherit the Scottish throne. The act required the King's principal subjects to sign a declaration of loyalty, which effectively committed them to Presbyterianism, Episcopalianism and Catholicism all at the same time. It was widely seen as an unworkable joke, and the Earl of Argyll, when signing, added the rider that he agreed with its content 'as far as it is consistent within itself'.

His comment was ill-advised. Apparently driven by his thwarted designs on Tobermory, James brought a charge of treason against the Earl. Argyll was convicted by a narrow majority and sentenced to death, but before his execution he escaped from Edinburgh Castle and fled to the Continent. On Charles II's death in 1685 James became King, and the exiled Argyll lent support to a new pretender to the throne, the Duke of Monmouth, whose abortive rebellion collapsed bloodily in 1685. The Earl was foolhardy enough to return to Scotland, where he was immediately arrested and beheaded.

On his exile, the Earl's property, including his rights to the wreck, had become forfeit to the Crown. Almost immediately James offered a salvage reward of 50 per cent to anyone who could recover the treasure. One of the applicants was Archibald Miller of Greenock, who had been one of James Mauld's divers in 1665. 'Though I be an old man,' enthused Miller in his prospectus of 1683, 'I am willing yet to go alone upon due consideration, for it is a pity that such a great business should be lost where it may be recovered by industry.' His assessment of the project provides us with another diver's-eye view of the wreck:

The Ship lyes Sunck off the Shore, about one-finger stone-cast, her Sterne lyes into the Shore Norwest ... There is no Deck upon her Except in ye Hinder part, there is one great heap of Timber wch I take to be the Cabbin, I did see one doore there wch I take to be the Steerage doore, and within that doore I did see a number of Dishes both great & small of a White blewish Colour, but whether they are pewter or plate I know not.

Neer this place I did see one great Gun & her Mussle upright on end, as big or bigger than the Gun I lifted wch would carry a 48 lb. ball, there is a great heap of Cannon shot about Midship, & upon the Shot lyes three Iron Gunns.

In the fore part of the Ship lyes many great Ballast stones & some shot amongst them, & there wee found one Silver bell about 4 li weight, wee got within the Ship at a prety distance the said great Gun wth other two (all Brass Gunns) the great Gun is eleaven feet length, & seaven inches & one fourth part of measure in the bore, th' other two were Minions, wee also got two Demy Culverins, two Falcons, two Slings all Brass.

We lifted three Anchors whereof one was eighteen feet of length, th' other was fifteen and the third was ten, I got two brass sheeves [pully wheels] weighing Sixty pounds, I lifted also the Rother [rudder], & took eight iron pykes [hinges] of it, It was twenty eight foot of Length, but there is no peece broken of the same.

I lifted the Kemp stone [capstan] of Curious worke, pauled with a Spring at every inches end, I cannot tell ye bigness, the thing I found would have been two foot in the Diameter.

I saw something like a Coat of Armes but could not reach it being entangled, I saw Guild [gilding] upon severall standing peeces of the Ship.

I found something like Mettle betwixt the Ship & shore in soft Osie ground in severall places & thinck they were Gunns.

with associated piles of roundshot, match observations made on other Armada wreck sites. And the enormous rudder, described as 28 ft (8.4 m) long, was certainly not an exaggeration. Recently the complete rudder of another Armada ship, the 860-ton *Juliana* (also of the Levant Squadron), was found off the Sligo coast. It measures 35 ft (10.5 m) from top to bottom.

But Archibald Miller added a couple of tit-bits, clearly intended to whet the appetites of potential sponsors. They include a 'paper of Lattin Extracted out of the Spanish Records that there was thirty millions of Cash on board the said Ship, and it tells it lay under ye Sell of the Gunroome'. This paper, if it ever existed, was clearly fictitious. There is no mention in Spain's systematic records of such a treasure aboard any of the Armada's ships. Finally, Miller's prospectus leaves a tantalizing but unconvincing glimpse of good things to come. On his last dive for Mauld, he avers, he 'found a Crowne or Diadem & had hooked the same, but being Chained it fell amongst the Timbers.'

In the event, the contract was given, in 1686, to four men – William Harrington, Richard Penclarvis, Cornelius de Gelder, and Samuel Souton. Over the course of the next three summers they worked on the wreck, recovering 12 more bronze guns but little else (**11**). It was

Most of Miller's account carries a ring of authenticity. The 'great Gun' standing upright among the wreckage, with its length of 11 feet and bore of 7¼ inches, was certainly one of the Gregorio Loeffer siege pieces, for which these specifications fit exactly. The ballast stones,

11 A bronze gun recovered from the Tobermory wreck, probably during the late seventeenth century. It is now at Inveraray Castle. The piece carries the salamander badge and initial of Francis I of France (d. 1547), and was probably captured by the Spaniards at the battle of Pavia (1525). Length 2.86 m (9 ft 4 in).

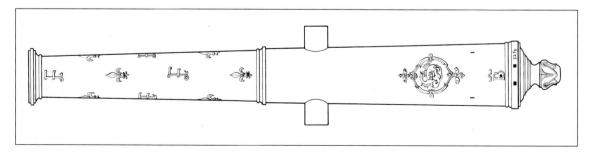

probably these divers who William Sacheverell watched 'sinking threescore Foot under Water, and stay sometimes an hour and at last returning with the spoils of the Ocean; whether it were Plate or Money'. In 1688 Sacheverell himself made an attempt on the wreck, but the weather defeated him – the 'whole Frame of nature seem'd inhospitable, black, Stormy, Rainy, Windy, so that our Divers could not bear the cold.' He consoled himself with a visit to Iona.

The 10th Earl of Argyll (who later became the first Duke) was more fortunate than his father and grandfather. Under William and Mary his lands and titles were restored, and he was free to search for the supposed treasure in Tobermory Bay. But by now the limits of bell salvage had probably been reached, and little more was achieved there during the next 40 years.

Jacob Rowe's diving engine

In 1720 Captain Jacob Rowe of London patented a remarkable diving 'engine' (**12**). The machine was a truncated vessel of brass or copper within which the diver lay prone. His arms protruded through sealed sleeves of copper and leather, and he looked down through a small glass porthole. A watertight lid provided entry. The apparatus was operated slightly head-up, to improve the diver's field of view and provide better arm-room when working on the bottom. It also prevented water from gathering around his face in the event of a leak.

A block of lead ballast was fastened beneath the apparatus, which was suspended by a rope from its mother craft. Communication with the surface was provided by a life-line. Buoyancy was adjusted so that the engine just sank, and this made it easy to haul it up at intervals to replenish the air by inserting bellows into bung holes on its top. For raising the machine clear of the water a block-and-tackle hoist was employed.

In effect the device was an armoured diving dress, although the differential between atmospheric pressure within the vessel and water pressure outside it would severely squeeze the diver's upper arms where they emerged from the sleeves. This naturally increased with depth. A further effect was a tendency for the diver's whole body to be pushed up against the top of the vessel, and a back saddle was provided to counter this.

Even at quite modest depths these discomforts would have been unpleasant and disorienting, yet it is clear that the device was used effectively in up to 10 fathoms (18 m) of water. But this depth was close to a diver's physiological limits. One of Rowe's men experienced a strong stricture in his arms at 11 fathoms (20 m), and that 'venturing two fathom lower to take up a lump of earth with Pieces of Eight sticking together; the circulation of his blood was so far stopped, and he suffered so much, that he was forced to keep his bed six weeks'. Another diver died after reaching 14 fathoms (26 m).

In 1727 Rowe and his partner William Evans had gone to Fair Isle to salvage the wreck of the Armada ship *El Gran Grifón* (see Chapter 2), and a year later they had become involved in the recovery of treasure from the Dutch East Indiaman *Adelaar* off Barra (see Chapter 5). But these ventures, though successful (especially the *Adelaar*) collapsed in litigation and huge debts. Rowe and his associate in the *Adelaar* venture, Alexander Mackenzie of Delvine, therefore decided on an attempt to revive their flagging fortunes by bringing the new diving technology to Tobermory.

John Campbell, the 2nd Duke of Argyll, was enthusiastic in his support, and in addition to agreeing to share the profits he offered to put up capital himself. Even Scotland's Lord Advocate, Duncan Forbes of Culloden, invested in the venture.

In 1729 Rowe and his men set to work. From the descriptions of the earlier salvors it was clear that much collapsed debris would need to be removed to gain entry to the wreck, while its deeper recesses – where they were confident the

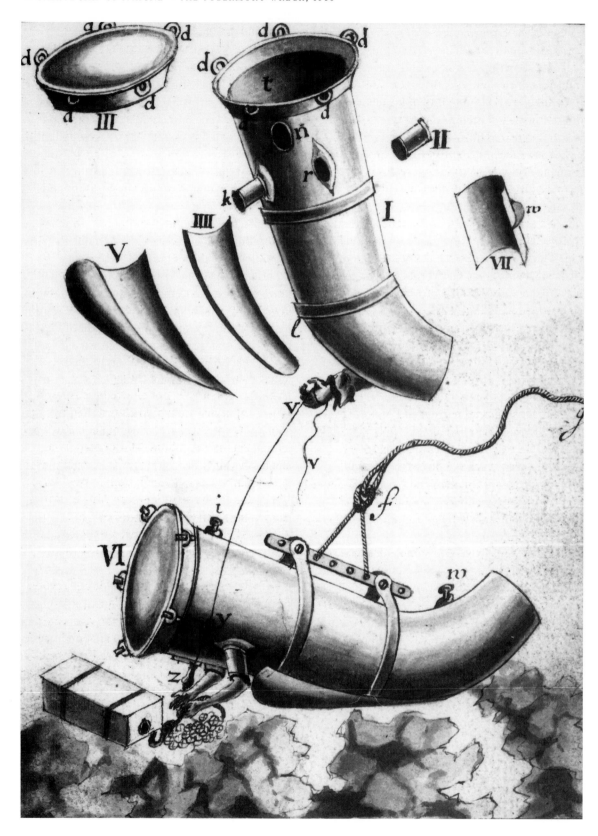

12 Captain Jacob Rowe's patented diving 'engine', from a
manuscript of 1720.

treasure lay – would best be reached by ripping the hull apart. This gargantuan task of destruction was accomplished with great ingenuity and determination.

Loose timbers were prised clear by the divers, using a variety of hand tools, and either dragged to one side or hauled to the surface. The shingle which filled the wreck was removed with buckets and dredges. Then the main structure was attacked. Some timbers were wrenched free by attaching them to rafts of barrels on the surface which, as the tide rose, exerted a pull equal to their buoyancy. The main frames of the ship were dragged apart with long cables attached to windlasses mounted on the shore. Barrels of explosives were set among the wreckage and detonated either with clockwork fuses or by means of red-hot iron balls dropped into them from the surface through wire-reinforced leather tubes.

Several months of this drastic treatment reduced the near-complete Ragusan argosy to not much more than the bottom of her hull. Here, surely, the treasure would be found. On 20 November Rowe wrote confidently to Alexander Mackenzie that

> we have been making as large a progress by way of Dragging or Clearing the Wreck as if it had been Summer Season, so that in the Spring Season when the Water is most clear and Fittest for Diving we shall have nothing more to do than clearing of wood and taking up Guns and Treasure.
>
> The Draggs under the Platform ... hath broken off considerable quantities of semented Cakes of Ballast, the under part of which bears the lively impression of Iron hoops of Casks and Chists, which I really judge to be Treasure, but by the hardness and smoothness thereof we have not been able to penetrate the same so far as to take up a Specimen, but I am continually endeavouring

to undermine it with our Dragg, which I hope to accomplish, but if I fail in the attempt, I have prepared a Machine that will break it all to pieces.

The machine was an explosive dart, and though it seems to have been effective in breaking through the crust of ballast and concretion it revealed beneath only iron shot. Rowe's backers were now beginning to desert him and, close to desperation, he turned his attention to the seabed surrounding the wreck. Here he found little except debris left by the earlier expeditions. Work was still going on in 1731, by which time it was clear that the wreck had little more to yield. Eventually Rowe departed for another (equally unproductive) venture in the Clyde, leaving debts and ruin behind him.

A lost heritage

What then has become of the legendary Tobermory treasure? It is elusive because it is illusory. The *San Juan de Sicilia* was an invasion transport, not a treasure galleon; her cargo was troops, munitions and the stuff of war. True, she had wealthy people aboard who would have with them some cash and personal valuables. No doubt much of this has been recovered over the years, together with most of the ship's guns. Almost all of what was left has probably been lost in the destructive processes of treasure-driven salvage.

In spite of the wreck's systematic destruction by Rowe and his predecessors, attempts to recover the imaginary treasure have continued into modern times. These were facilitated by the invention of the closed diving dress in the mid nineteenth century. In 1871 a diver called Gush investigated the site, but nearly came to grief when his air-line parted. Thirty years later his son participated in an expedition mounted by the Glasgow Salvage Association, which brought a steam dredger to the site. Among the tons of silt brought to the surface a number of artefacts were found, and later dispersed by sale. A few survive in private hands today (13).

13 A breech-loading swivel gun recovered from the Tobermory wreck c.1900, and now in a private collection. Length 1.38 m (4 ft 6 in).

14 Margaret Naylor, 'Britain's first woman diver', at Tobermory in 1924.

Between 1909 and 1932 a remarkable eccentric, Colonel Kenneth Mackenzie Foss, mounted a sustained attempt to locate the treasure. With considerable backing, and a sound practical approach to the engineering aspects of the enterprise, he systematically removed the silts which had accumulated since Jacob Rowe's efforts. Some objects from the wreck – coins, pottery, pewter plates, and a silver medallion – were recovered. Operations were curtailed by World War I, but

recommenced in 1922 with fresh backing. A modest trickle of small finds continued – many of them broken by the brutal recovery methods employed – but of the expected treasure there was not a trace.

Convinced that his men were concealing finds from him Foss taught his 26-year-old secretary, Margaret Naylor, to dive (**14**). Her venture into what had previously been an exclusively male preserve caused a sensation in the press, but her discoveries were no more spectacular than those of her colleagues. By 1927 Foss had become deranged by his obsession, and was advocating impossible schemes to raise the ship and convey her round the world as a floating exhibition. Five years later the Duke of Argyll politely informed him that he did not 'wish any further correspondence as to the Tobermory Galleon'.

There have been other hopefuls since. In 1950s a noted naval diver, Commander 'Buster' Crabb (who later disappeared in mysterious circumstances during the visit of Bulganin and Kruschev to Britain in 1956), negotiated an agreement between the Duke of Argyll and the Admiralty whereby two naval vessels came to Tobermory to search for the wreck. The operation was a fiasco which ended in awkward parliamentary questions as to why taxpayers' money was being used to sponsor a private treasure hunt. Another expedition involving naval personnel (but not equipment) was launched in 1975, with equally predictable results. The most recent attempt was made in 1982. Among many other optimistic schemes which have come to nought was one proposed by a consortium of Florida dentists.

There is no treasure of the conventional kind to be found in Tobermory Bay, because that was not the nature of the *San Juan de Sicilia's* cargo. Sadly the real treasure would have been the ship herself, frozen as a sixteenth- century time-capsule with its varied contents wonderfully preserved within this sheltered oxygen-free environment. Had the wreck been left in peace two Campbell chiefs would have kept their heads, almost as much money as is alleged to have gone down with the ship might have been saved, and dozens of enterprising and capable individuals (and not a few charlatans) would have been spared disillusion and ruin.

Such a monument would rank today as a national treasure to rival the *Vasa* or the *Mary Rose*. But little now remains of the *San Juan de Sicilia* save perhaps the lower part of her hull – though even this, as the only known fragment of a Ragusan argosy to survive anywhere in the world, would still be worthy of preservation and protection for future generations.

The days of indiscriminate underwater treasure-hunting are over, for it is an unrewarding, destructive and essentially selfish pursuit. Historic shipwrecks are now protected as significant ancient monuments in their own right. The fragile riches which lie beneath our seas are archaeological ones, and they are a heritage too precious to lose.

2
Cave of the Tide Race –
El Gran Grifón, 1588

'Ane schipe full of Spainyertis ...'

At daybreak on 6 December 1588 one of the town bailies woke the minister of Anstruther, the Reverend James Melville, from his slumbers (**15**). A large ship had anchored in the harbour, he reported, and it was full of Spanish soldiers. Their officers, continued the agitated official, had come ashore, but had been ordered back to their ship until the magistrates could be consulted. 'Up I got with diligence,' continued Melville in his diary,

15 James Melville's manse in Anstruther. It was built some years after his encounter with the survivors from *El Gran Grifón* in 1588.

and assembling the honest men of the town, came to the Tolbooth; and after consultation taken to hear them, and what answer to make, there presents to us a very reverend man of big stature, of grave and stout countenance, grey-haired and very humble like, who, after muckle and very low courtesy, bowing down with his face near the ground, and twitching my shoe with his hand, began his harangue in the Spanish tongue.

This polite and distinguished stranger introduced himself as Juan Gomez de Medina, one-time governor of Cadiz, whose ship *El Gran Grifón* had been wrecked two months earlier on Fair Isle. The 650-ton *Grifón* had been flagship of the Spanish Armada's 23-strong supply squadron which he commanded. She was a tubby Baltic hulk built at the Hanseatic League port of Rostock, high-charged and bluff-bowed (**16**). The crest of this quasi-independent city-state was a rampant griffin (eagle-headed lion), from which the ship took her name. Most of the other vessels in the squadron were also Baltic hulks (an exception was the *Santo Andres*, which came from Dundee). These capacious but clumsy cargo ships carried troops, provisions, munitions and some livestock – horses and mules for the artillery train – but they were not front-line fighting vessels.

They had nevertheless been vital to the Spanish war effort, and were an important contribution to the Armada itself. In the two years prior to the campaign, Baltic hulks had been active in transporting naval stores from northern Europe to Philip II's strategic ports of Lisbon and Cadiz. These cargoes included masts and spars, tar, rope and – increasingly – cast-iron artillery from the new foundries of Germany and Sweden. *El Gran Grifón* had herself arrived with such a consignment at San Lucar, the harbour at the mouth of the Guadalquivir below Cadiz, in March 1587, when she was embargoed to take part in the forthcoming Armada. In due course she sailed to Lisbon where the fleet was assembling.

16 A Baltic hulk similar to *El Gran Grifón* (engraving after Brueghel).

'This day of our great peril'

On 7 May 1588 the Armada's commander, the Duke of Medina Sidonia, held a grand muster of his fleet. *El Gran Grifón* was confirmed as flagship of the hulks, and credited with an armament of 38 guns. Most were relatively light – 5-pounders or less – and were made of wrought or cast iron. These were evidently the ship's own weapons, carried to protect her on the high seas as she went about her mercantile endeavours. Such weapons were essentially anti-personnel pieces, which at close range could cause havoc on an enemy's decks but were too light to inflict serious structural damage on a ship's hull. At Lisbon she had taken a further eight pieces aboard, all of bronze. Four were *medias sacres* – long, light pieces which fired 3-

pound iron balls. The other four were *medias culebrinas*, or demi-culverins, which were slender 9-pounders designed to deliver ship-smashing blows into an enemy's hull. Fifty solid iron balls were provided for each piece, together with 48 *quintales* (2200 kg/4800 lb) of gunpowder. This was fine-grained so that it could also be used for the small-arms carried by the troops.

In addition to her general cargo of invasion stores the *Grifón* carried 286 men. Forty-three were from the ship's original crew – mostly Germans from Rostock under the vessel's owner and master, Burgat Querquerman. The remainder were Spanish or Italian soldiers, 243 in all, together with their company officers Patricio Antolinez, Pedro Hurtado de Corcuera and Esteban de Legorreta.

During the battles in the English Channel *El Gran Grifón* was hotly engaged on at least two occasions. On 3 August she was singled out by a front-line English warship – probably Drake's *Revenge* – and given several devastating broadsides. Fifty or more of her people were killed, and she sustained severe damage to her hull. Even so, the Englishman declined to close and board the wounded hulk because the *Grifón's* bloody decks were thronged with 200 determined and well-trained soldiers who wished for nothing better than to get within sword's length of their elusive tormentors.

Eventually the *Grifón* was extricated from the mêlée and brought into the midst of the fleet, where she was able to make emergency repairs. The ship is next heard of on 8 August in the confused battle which followed the scattering of the Armada by the English fireship attack off Calais. Though many of the ships panicked and fled, a core of stalwarts, including the *Grifón*, rallied on Medina Sidonia's flagship to fight the rearguard action which saved the fleet from grounding on the Flemish sandbanks and allowed it to regroup for the long voyage home around the north of Scotland.

For a while *El Gran Grifón* kept up with the main body but, after the retreating Armada had rounded Orkney, her poor sailing performance, exacerbated by battle-damage, caused her to fall behind. At first she struggled on in the company of three other ships, two of them sister-hulks, the *Barca de Amburg* and the *Castillo Negro*. The third vessel was *La Trinidad Valencera*, later to be wrecked off Donegal. On 1 September the *Barca de Amburg*, her seams open and her pumps choked, signalled that she was foundering. Her company of 250 was transferred to the *Grifón* and *Valencera* just before she sank.

Three nights later, somewhere off the north-west coast of Ireland, the remaining ships lost contact. Alone, and in almost continually adverse weather, *El Gran Grifón* beat south-westwards into the Atlantic until on 7 September a great storm fell on her causing the hull's weakened seams to open up – some of them, we are told, gaping a hand's breadth apart. An oncoming sea would now sink her, and she had no choice but to run with the weather.

Harrowing details of her final days are preserved in the journal of one of the survivors. Though it is unsigned, the account may well be that of Juan Gomez de Medina himself. The diarist records how for three days they ran northwards until they reached 'an island of Scotland of about 37½ degrees latitude'. This must have been St Kilda. Then the wind veered unexpectedly to the north-east, allowing the almost helpless vessel to turn once more 'towards our dear Spain'. For three days the favourable wind held, carrying the ship to the latitude of Galway Bay. But then it backed once again into the prevailing south-west quarter. Our diarist once more takes up the story: 'We turned back and sailed for three days more to the latitude we had been in before. But when we got there we were fit only to die, for the wind was so strong and the sea so wild that the waves mounted to the skies.'

The exhausted Spaniards toiled ceaselessly at the pumps, and attempted to patch up the worst of the leaks with oxhides and planks. By 25

September they had sighted the Hebrides, at which point they decided to make for the nearest land, even if it meant running the hulk ashore. Somehow they negotiated the Orkney archipelago by night, apparently aided by the glow of the Northern Lights ('God in his mercy at that moment sent us a vivid gleam through the dark night').

On the morning of 27 September, with the ship now wallowing almost uncontrollably with ten feet of water in her hold, Fair Isle was sighted. At dusk Gomez de Medina anchored 'in a sheltered spot we found, this day of our great

17 Air photograph of the *Gran Grifón* wreck site at Stroms Hellier, Fair Isle.

peril, 27 September 1588'. The next day *El Gran Grifón* drove ashore. She fetched up against the overhanging cliff of Stroms Hellier – the Cave of the Tide Race – close to the south-eastern corner of the island (**17**). There she wedged fast. Most of those on board escaped by climbing ashore up the foremast, which lay against the overhang, but seven perished in the attempt and little apart from portable valuables could be saved from the ship.

Local tradition records how the grimly attired soldiery, cautiously advancing through the mist, were mistaken by the islanders for the Heavenly Host, who thought that the Day of Judgement had arrived! The situation was a delicate one because Fair Isle was small and storm-bound, and there was little immediate prospect of escape. With winter approaching, the island families had little to spare for the hungry castaways who, to their credit, made no attempt to seize the islanders' provisions by force. Later stories of suspicion and treachery between the two parties appear to be without foundation. On the contrary, a report later sent to Philip II noted that 'a gentleman of rank [Gomez de Medina] was in the Scottish islands, where the people were very much pleased with him, as he paid well for everything he had of them.'

The journey home

The survivor's journal provides a remarkable description of Fair Isle and its people in the late sixteenth century, albeit from the somewhat condescending perspective of a Spanish grandee:

> We found the island peopled by seventeen households in huts, more like hovels than anything else. They are savage people, whose usual food is fish, without bread, except for a few barley-meal bannocks cooked over the embers of a fuel they use, which they make or extract from the earth and call turf. They have some cattle, quite enough for themselves, for they rarely eat meat. They depend mainly upon the milk and butter from their cows, using their sheep's wool principally for clothing. They are a very dirty people, neither Christians nor altogether heretics.

After six weeks of privation on the island during which some 50 of their number died, including the ship's captain Burgat Querquerman, the Spaniards managed to reach Quendale at the southern tip of Shetland. There, after staying for three weeks under the protection of the local laird, Malcolm Sinclair, they engaged a Scottish ship which brought them to Anstruther and their encounter with the Reverend James Melville. After enduring a lengthy Calvinist sermon on the error of their ways, Gomez de Medina and his officers were spirited away to be entertained by the local gentry, while the soldiers and mariners were 'suffered to come to land, and lie all together, to the number of thirteen score, for the most part young beardless men, silly, trauchled, and hungered, to the which kail, porridge, and fish was given'.

Four days later the Spaniards crossed the Forth to Leith, where their arrival caused a considerable stir. In an age when news travelled slowly, and was difficult to verify, rumours abounded. One claimed that the Armada was undefeated, and Spanish landings were reported at Dunbar, St Andrews, Aberdeen and the Cromarty Firth. These proved to be false alarms, but many wrecked survivors were on the loose in Scotland. They included the company of troops from the Tobermory ship, still causing havoc in the Western Isles. Another contingent had arrived from two wrecks off Norway. From Ireland, too, came a pathetic dribble of fugitives from the terrible wreckings and massacres which had occurred along its wild Atlantic coast.

The presence of Spanish troops on Scottish soil was an embarrassment to the young king, James VI. Although Scotland was technically neutral in the conflict between England and Spain, he had expectations of succeeding to Elizabeth's throne when she died, and he had no wish to provoke her displeasure. The situation was complicated by the presence of a strong pro-Spanish faction in Scotland, mostly Catholic though it included unprincipled Protestants like the Earl of Bothwell who were playing for the high political stakes. Juan Gomez de Medina, as the highest-ranking Spanish officer to reach Scotland, was naturally a target for intrigue. At the beginning of January 1589 an English agent reported that 'Don John de Medina and diverse captains of the Spaniards are going hence with great credit ... On Sunday last I dined with Bothwell, where I found four Spanish captains whom he entertained.'

By then Gomez de Medina was on the point of departing in a 40-ton barque provided by Bothwell's agent, Colonel Stewart, with an exhortation to 'let the Spanish king know how many well-wishers he hath in this country, and to procure but 4,000 Spaniards, good shot, and leaders, with a sum of money to be brought hither by his conduct with speed.' In fact there was little likelihood of such Spanish involvement ever materializing. Philip II had no wish to become embroiled in the internal politics of a remote and (to his eyes) insignificant kingdom on the fringes of Europe, and had issued his men with clear instructions to avoid them. As for the survivors themselves, their overwhelming desire was to return home, and Gomez de Medina's swift departure appears to have been motivated by no more than a good officer's concern to expedite the repatriation of his men.

There were formidable difficulties to overcome. Some 600 Spaniards were now gathered at Leith, but they were short of money and ten shillings a head was demanded for their passage to Flanders. Understandably they also refused to sail unless their safety was guaranteed should they put in to an English port on the way. Queen Elizabeth prevaricated about providing the necessary safe conduct and, concerned about the security of her northern border, dispatched three warships to patrol the entrance to the Forth. In July two big galleons, the *Vanguard* and the *Tiger*, anchored off Leith. In less troubled times this might have been regarded as a high-handed act against a neighbouring friendly state, but the English officers were warmly received by King James at Holyrood, and passes were given to the seamen to come ashore and sample the pleasures of the capital.

Trouble was not long in following. After carousing fraternally with Scots and Spaniards in a dockside tavern, harsh words were evidently exchanged, and in the ensuing fracas an English trumpeter was fatally stabbed by a Spanish soldier. The diplomatic turmoil which ensued threatened the whole delicate process of negotiating the Spaniards' repatriation.

Early in August, however, Elizabeth unexpectedly granted a safe conduct for the Spaniards in all English ports, and money was found for their passage to Dunkirk. Safety apparently thus assured, the 600 Armada survivors embarked in four Scottish ships. While they progressed down the eastern coast of England, Elizabeth's guarantees were scrupulously observed, but a deadly trap was about to be sprung. When it was in sight of Dunkirk, the convoy was pounced upon by a fleet of rebel Dutch gunboats. The Queen's safe conduct had studiously omitted to mention her Protestant allies on the Continent.

One ship was captured and everyone on board, Scotsman and Spaniard alike, was peremptorily thrown over the side. The three other vessels ran ashore in an effort to escape and broke up in the surf under heavy fire from the gunboats. More than half of the remaining Spaniards perished.

Yet the story has an unexpected and humane postscript. A year or so after the Armada scare had died away, James Melville, the Anstruther minister, records in his diary how Gomez de Medina, on returning to Cadiz in Colonel Stewart's barque,

showed great kindness to a ship of our town, which he found arrested on his homecoming, went to court for her, and spoke on behalf of Scotland to his king, took the honest men to his house, and enquired for the laird of Anstruther, for the minister, and his host, and sent home many commendations.

A few Armada survivors remained in Scotland, considering themselves to be 'better entertained [as servants in noblemen's houses] than they look to be, in following the wars'. Some no doubt married local girls. Traditions of such

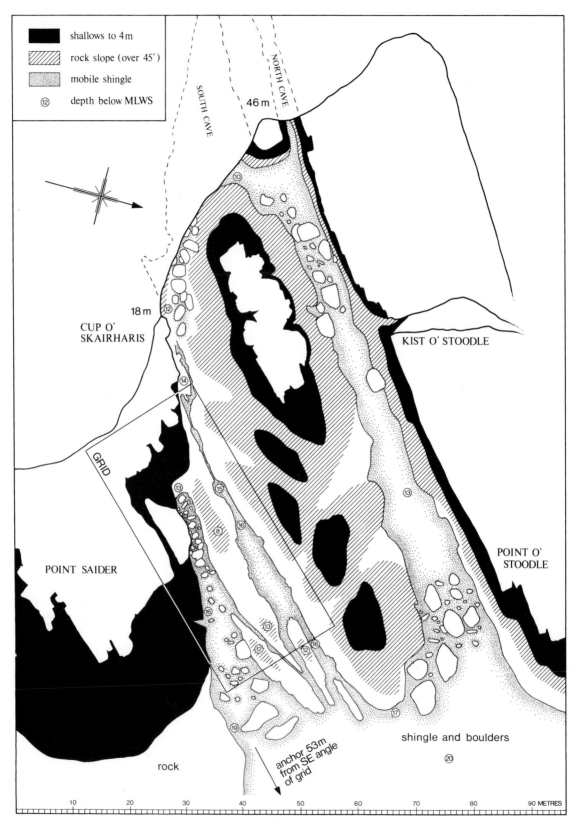

18 The underwater topography of Stroms Hellier. Most
    of the wreckage is contained within the rectangle
    marked 'Grid'.

ancestry persist in a number of Scottish families,
though none has ever been proved.

Early salvage

Stroms Hellier is a deep wedge-shaped inlet
formed by the collapse of two caves which
penetrate Fair Isle's south-eastern cliffs. Its
overhanging apex rises nearly 50 m (160 ft)
above the surviving cave mouths, and its centre
is dominated by a reef which splits the inlet into
two deep gullies. At the head of the inlet the reef
breaks the surface as a long ragged rock, once
believed in local tradition to be the fossilized
hull of the wrecked ship. Although this is
patently untrue, the supposition was based on
an accurate folk-memory of the wreck's
location, because the archaeological remains of
El Gran Grifón lie at the foot of this reef,
among the gullies which run below its south-
eastern edge (18).

The ship evidently lodged between the reef
and the shore, in such a position as to allow the
survivors to scramble up the foremast and onto
the cliff top. They were able to bring their
valuables with them (a later report from
Edinburgh noted that 'they saved their treasure
and are come hither unspoiled'), and it is likely
that much more was salvaged from the hulk
before it sank – if not by Spaniards then by the
islanders, who would scarcely have let so rich an
opportunity pass. Only the munitions and
provisions in the flooded hold would have been
beyond their reach, while it may be imagined
that the big guns on the upper decks defied any
attempt to swing them up the cliff. When the
ship eventually broke apart these heavy items
fell to the gully floor, some 15 m (50 ft) below.

Within five years of the wrecking the
notorious Earl Patrick of Orkney signed a
contract with William Irvine of Seabay to
'address himself ... unto the Fair Isle and there,
with all means possible, shall win the ordnance

that was lost there in the Spanish ship'. Whether
this was attempted, or with what success, is not
known. Some further efforts at salvage appear
to have been made in the seventeenth century.

In 1727 a partnership was drawn up between
Captain Jacob Rowe and William Evans to fit
out a vessel 'with the proper engines for diving
upon and recovering a wreck supposed to be
lying near the island called the Fair Island'.
Rowe had patented an ingenious diving 'engine'
(see p. 23–24), and was seeking treasure-laden
shipwrecks within its working depth of about
18 m (60 ft). Their intention on Fair Isle was to
'raise a Spanish ship, or man of war, called the
Grand Admiral of Spain (and one of the Spanish
Armada) mounted with 130 brass guns or
thereabouts'. Rowe and Evans had confused
their wreck with the Armada's overall flagship
San Martín, which had returned safely to Spain
with the Duke of Medina Sidonia. Gomez de
Medina's name was obviously the source of the
misconception (in fact he was distantly related
to Medina Sidonia), but even then they were
wildly optimistic about the number of guns
aboard. The *San Martín* had carried only 48
pieces, not 130.

In ignorance of these dispiriting facts the two
adventurers set to work with gusto, and on 28
July 1728 it was reported that 'the company of
divers on Fair Isle have found the wreck of one
of the Spanish Armada and have got 2 or 3
brass cannons and talk of a great prospect they
have there of no less than 40 or £50,000 stg'. A
later report confirmed the recovery of two brass
guns 'of a large size' together with 'some other
articles of a less value'. The two guns were in
due course shipped to Leith, and their
subsequent fate is unknown.

The operations in Stroms Hellier were
hazardous, and at least one man was killed. By the
beginning of August, moreover, it had become
clear that the wreck was unlikely to yield much of
value. At this point news of the *Adelaar's*
wrecking on Barra reached Fair Isle, and Rowe
and Evans resolved to cut their losses in favour of
richer pickings elsewhere (see Chapter 6).

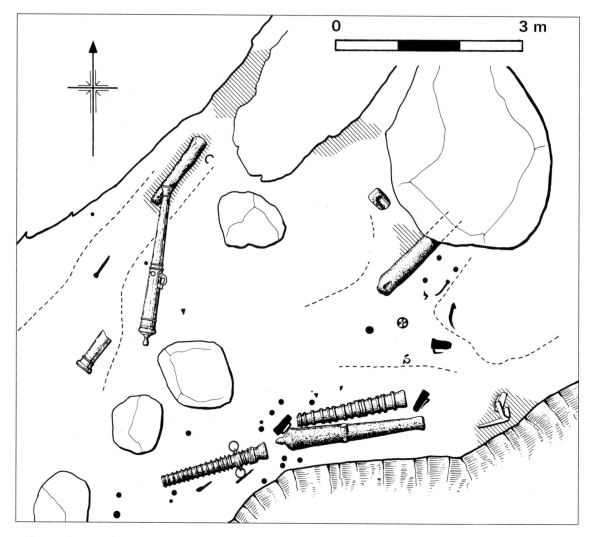

19 Part of the excavated area on *Gran Grifón* wreck site, showing iron and bronze guns together with various small finds.

These were the last diving operations in Stroms Hellier until modern times, though the site of the wreck continued to be remembered in island tradition and in about 1770 it was reported that 'a ship bolt, long and thick, was thrown ashore in a neighbouring gulf'.

The wreck site today

In 1970 the author and his colleagues Sydney Wignall, Chris Oldfield, and Simon Martin explored the site at Stroms Hellier as part of a wider study into the archaeology of the Spanish Armada. Following information provided by Mr Jerry Stout of Leogh, a nearby croft, the wreck was located without difficulty. The first indication was the muzzle of a bronze gun protruding from the shingle at the foot of the cliff close to the south-western edge of the inlet, at a depth of 16 m (52 ft). Its bore was 7.5 cm (3¼ in), which identified it as one of the four 3-pounder *medias sacres* consigned to the ship at Lisbon shortly before she sailed. Close to it were three iron guns.

These finds were contained within a broad gully which tapers towards the shore, ending in a rising tumble of boulders (**19**). Beyond this gully is a narrower one running along the south-eastern edge of Stroms Hellier's central spine. At its head the cleft in the rock, worn smooth by the attrition of moving shingle, reduces to little more than a diver's width. In here lay another iron gun, so heavily abraded that its bore was sectioned along its full length. At the breech end a cannon ball was still in place.

Nearby lay six lead ingots, of a kind used by the Spanish soldiery for casting bullets (**20**). Scattered among the pockets of shingle were numerous dull-grey lead balls of musket and arquebus calibre – 20 and 13 mm (¾ and ½ in) in diameter respectively. Of the structure of the ship there was no trace.

Later searches beyond the mouth of Stroms Hellier revealed an anchor, almost certainly belonging to the ship, in deep water some 60 m (200 yds) to the south-east. It had probably been dropped in an attempt to control the ship as she was being driven ashore.

The remainder of the 1970 investigation was taken up by survey and limited excavation. Survey and recording are carried out underwater in much the same way as on land. Fixed datum points are established, usually by driving climbers' pitons into cracks in the rock, and these are used to build up a network of reference points by fixing their relative positions by triangulation with measuring tapes. Once these points have been established they can be

used to locate grids of various sizes, from which scale drawings are made on waterproof drafting film (**colour plate 2**). As the survey progresses the disparate elements are brought together to create an archaeological plan.

To remove the shingle which overlies the wreck deposits an air lift is employed. This consists of a long pipe which extends from the seabed to the surface. Air pumped to the lower end of the pipe from a compressor on shore mixes with water to form a frothy emulsion which rises to the surface, creating a suction which carries with it stones, shingle and sand (**21**). Used carefully, this can transport spoil from an archaeological deposit in much the same way that a terrestrial excavator removes overburden with a wheelbarrow or even a mechanical excavator.

The isolation of archaeological features underwater is done as carefully as on land. Instead of a brush or trowel, however, the digger's hand is usually the best implement, for by generating water movement in the right direction sediments can be displaced with precise control. The merest waggle of the fingers

20 Lead ingots recovered from the wreck. They were used for casting shot, and making repairs to the ship. Scale in inches.

21 A suction-pipe, or 'air lift', used for removing spoil from the site.

22 A silver 4-*real* coin of Philip II, minted at Toledo.

is all that is required for delicate work, while more vigorous fanning with the open palm allows quite substantial quantities of spoil to be shifted quickly. Once displaced, the spoil can be fed into the air lift and deposited in a suitable location clear of the excavation area.

The 1970 excavation yielded a few finds – more iron guns, roundshot, abraded fragments of copper and pewter utensils, and a silver coin (22). Also found was the muzzle-end of a larger bronze gun, whose calibre of 11 cm (4¼ in) identified it as one of the ship's 9-pounder *medias culebrinas*. The cork muzzle-plug had been driven some distance into the barrel, presumably by water pressure as the gun sank, which suggests that the barrel was intact when it went down. Apart from this item no organic material of any kind was encountered, while a few iron bolts and a rudder pintle were all that remained of the *Grifón's* 650-ton hull (23).

These excavations were confined to the base of the cliff, where the first finds had been made, and it was suspected that more significant

23 One of *El Gran Grifón's* rudder pintles.

archaeological deposits lay in the gully immediately below the central reef. An expedition to investigate this gully was mounted in 1977 by the Scottish Institute of Maritime Studies at St Andrews University. Its intention was to remove the shingle down to bedrock, layer by layer, so that archaeological features could be identified and recorded in their stratigraphical contexts. This involved removing some 200 cubic metres – about 400 tonnes – of loose overburden and boulders.

An air lift was rigged to discharge spoil into the gully on the far side of the reef, thus avoiding the possibility of Stroms Hellier's heavy surges refilling the excavated areas. Trial digging revealed that there was no archaeological material whatsoever in the 2 m (6ft) or so of loose shingle which filled the top part of the gully. It was clear that this shingle was in a state of fairly constant movement, being displaced and turned over from top to bottom during storms. Only at the very foot of the shingle deposit, in the narrowing V of the

gully bottom, had archaeologically stable levels survived (**24**).

The main feature was a solid raft of concretion which filled the gully bottom from side to side. Its top surface was flat and smooth, and flecked with silvery discs up to about 10 cm (4 in) in diameter. These proved to be cross-sections of cannon balls locked within concretion which had been worn down by the abrasive effects of moving shingle. The fact that the iron surfaces were free of rust shows that this process was constant and continuous. It may be presumed that in due course nature would have ground away the entire concreted deposit in the gully bottom. How much has been lost since 1588 is impossible to calculate.

Towards the middle of the gully a cast-iron gun had been sectioned in the same way, revealing in crisp detail its elaborate mouldings and part of its bore. Further inshore a large

24 A section through the main gully, showing how wreckage has stabilized towards the bottom. Level 1 is mobile shingle; 2 is partially stabilized shingle, stained by the concretion underneath; 3 incorporates a bronze gun and associated lead shot lying on top of the concretion; 4 is a matrix of concretion containing iron shot and broken pieces of guns; 5 is organic sludge; and 6 is shingle. 5 is probably decayed seaweed and other material sealed by the arrival of wreckage in 1588.

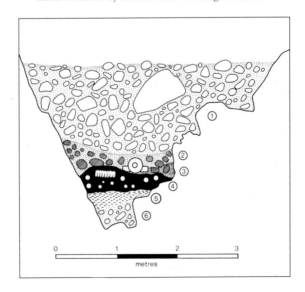

25 Lifting the bronze *media culebrina*, which weighs about a ton, with flotation bags.

bronze gun, its muzzle broken off, lay atop the concretion. This matched the muzzle-end which had been found previously in the neighbouring gully (**25 and colour plate 3**). The top surface of the concretion also revealed large quantities of lead shot, rolling loosely on it in a relatively unabraded condition. As the gully narrowed towards the cave at its apex, more lead shot was found, concentrated in rocky pockets adjacent to the six lead ingots.

These observations provide clues as to how *El Gran Grifón* broke up, and explain how her remains subsequently became incorporated into the seabed. Trapped in Stroms Hellier's south-eastern cleft, with her upper parts stripped of most of their moveable contents by contemporary salvors, the ship had quickly disintegrated. Some of the timbers probably floated away, while even the waterlogged ones which sank are unlikely to have survived long in so dynamic an environment.

All the heavy objects that remained – guns, roundshot, lead ingots and metal fittings – cascaded to the sea floor and gravitated to the gully bottoms. Those that landed among the shingle would at first have lain on its surface, but as the shingle shifted during storms, the material would have trended downwards until eventually it stabilized close to the bedrock.

As the buried iron corroded, the products of its decomposition formed a strong cement which bound together sand, stones, shells and the objects themselves into the durable concretion which has encapsulated and preserved them. Only the slow but inexorable attrition of the shifting shingle above continued to grind away at the top surface of the deposit.

These processes explain why some categories of material have *not* survived on the wreck site. We have already seen why organic objects have not been preserved, but what of more durable artefacts, such as pottery? There was certainly a good deal of this aboard *El Gran Grifón*. Her supplies of olive oil, for example, were shipped in distinctive round-bottomed earthenware jars – 588 of them, each containing about 6 litres (11 pints) (**6**). Cheap crockery in sets of four had also been issued to the troops. Yet not a single potsherd was found during the excavation.

The explanation seems to be that pottery, unlike metal, is about the same density as shingle. Potsherds would therefore have behaved as components of the shingle overburden, churning around in the mobile sediments as they were displaced during storms. Such material would never stabilize, and in time would be ground to nothing.

Other movements of archaeological material seem to have taken place after the concretion layer had been formed. The broken bronze gun which was found lying on its top surface had, presumably, not arrived until the concretion was solid and unyielding, a process which must have taken several years. Moreover, this gun was separated from its broken muzzle by about 10 m (32 ft) so if – as argued above – the breakage did not take place until the object hit the sea floor, then at least one of the parts must have moved that distance after the initial deposition.

The distribution of lead shot is also revealing. Most of it was trapped in fissures at the narrow shoreward end of the gully, but significant quantities lay on *top* of the concretion below the shingle. Like the bronze *media culebrina*, they must have arrived after the concretion had formed. Water movement had evidently, at some point, carried them from further up the gully.

The flow required to shift such heavy objects is high, and for most of the time no strong currents are encountered in the gully bottoms. But in storm conditions the situation is quite different. When a south-easterly sea is running, waves pile into the wedge-shaped cleft of Stroms Hellier, often rising halfway or more up its sides. This enormous hanging mass of water then dissipates its energy by falling and transferring its volume back to sea level. On such occasions the surge of water through the gullies must be phenomenal. This undoubtedly causes the violent movements evident in the mobile shingle in the gully bottoms, the constant grinding down of the concretion deposit, and the transportation of heavy objects across the site.

Archaeological conclusions

The discovery of so much roundshot on this site, as well as on other Armada wrecks, has been of profound interest to historians. It was widely believed that by the final stages of the campaign the Spaniards ran out of ammunition, and that this was one of the main reasons behind their failure. These finds clearly indicate that this was not the case. Because most of *El Gran Grifón's* munitions and guns became encapsulated in Stroms Hellier's enclosed gully system a large proportion of them has probably been recovered. For example, almost half of the 200 pieces of 9-pounder shot supplied for her four *medias culebrinas* have been found on the wreck site, which means that at least half of the heavy ship-smashing shot available was *not* fired at the English. The true figure is certainly higher, because it is unlikely that all the surviving pieces of shot have been recovered, while an unknowable number has probably been destroyed by natural attrition. For whatever reason *El Gran Grifón's* four largest guns – the only ones capable of inflicting serious damage on an adversary's hull – had, at best, been grossly under-used or, at worst, scarcely used at all.

As a result of recent archaeological discoveries it is becoming clear that in 1588 the

Spaniards experienced great difficulty in working their larger guns at sea. The Armada engagement was the first naval conflict in history in which artillery was the dominant arm and the shots – quite literally – were being called by the English. Elizabeth's galleons were mobile weapons platforms which utilized superior speed and manoeuvrability to dictate the range and direction of their attacks. They exploited this advantage to ply their artillery to best effect, and had developed compact and easily-handled carriages with four solid wheels which allowed the guns to be reloaded and fired in a continuous cycle.

The Spaniards, on the other hand, regarded their artillery as a secondary arm, the main purpose of which was to deliver a single broadside at close range to cripple and confuse an enemy in the vital seconds before a boarding assault was launched. If successful, this tactic was devastating, for Spanish troops were the best in the world and the Armada's ships were packed with them. Unfortunately for Spain, the nimble English galleons declined to come sufficiently close, but chose to stand off at the range that suited them best, close enough to deliver sustained gunfire but not so close as to risk being boarded.

This tactic threw the Spanish gun-crews, which were made up largely of soldiers, into disarray. Their guns, mounted on clumsy two-wheeled carriages, were ill-adapted for shipboard reloading under battle conditions, and in any case the troops had not been trained to carry out the necessary drills. These difficulties were exacerbated by an almost total lack of standardization in gun and shot sizes, muddle caused by the use of several different standards of weights and measures, and a confused system of command in which little co-operation existed between the soldiers and seamen. On top of this many of the guns were technically flawed.

A revealing example of the latter problem is provided by the bronze *media culebrina* recovered from *El Gran Grifón*. It is bored so far off centre that in all probability it had never been

26 The *media culebrina's* off-centre bore, revealed in its broken-off muzzle. Scale in inches.

fired, for even a much-reduced charge would certainly have blown out its weakened breech (**26**). Nor does this seem to have been an isolated case. The English gunner Robert Norton, writing in the early seventeenth century, noted of Spanish and Italian artillery that:

> it is apparent that they commit great and absurd faults therein. Some of their pieces (and not a few) are bored awry … [such guns] will either break, split, or blowingly spring their metals, and (besides the mischief they do) they will be utterly unserviceable ever after.

We know a good deal about the eight bronze guns issued to *El Gran Grifón* in late 1587 and early 1588. They were among a batch cast at Lisbon under the supervision of Philip II's Captain-General of Artillery, Juan de Acuña Vela, as part of a crash programme of gunfounding to help bring the Armada's armament up to strength. Corners were cut to speed up production, and special permission was granted by the King to dispense with the normally mandatory royal arms on the breeches. As both *Grifón* examples show, this dispensation was put into effect (**27**).

But lack of skill on the part of the gunfounders – one of them, an Italian called Bartolomé de Somorriva, was singled out for particular criticism – led to serious difficulties. One piece exploded during testing, killing two artillerymen and blowing the arm off another. Several other guns were rejected for erratic boring. When it is remembered that the eccentrically-bored *media culebrina* from *El Gran Grifón* was presumably passed as fit for service, those that were not must have been quite spectacularly faulty.

But even if bored true, these guns were open to further criticism. The thinness of their barrel walls made them prone to splitting, while their great length made them difficult to operate aboard ship. A contemporary Spanish drawing shows a *media culebrina* of almost exactly the same proportions as the *Grifón* example, with an annotated comment explicitly stating these criticisms. Below is shown a projected development in which, by shortening and thickening the piece, these problems could be solved without adding any weight. Unfortunately for *El Gran Grifón*'s gunners these sensible rationalizations came too late to help the Armada.

The wreck has also produced a number of the small iron guns the ship had carried as a Hanseatic merchantman (**28**). Some of these were wrought-iron, made up of strips and bands like the staves and hoops of a barrel. Such guns were based on medieval technologies which were becoming obsolete by 1588. All of them were breech-loading, with a detachable chamber which held the powder charge and was wedged into place before firing.

More modern were the cast-iron types, of which the wreck has produced several examples. The industrial skills necessary to make big iron castings were at an early stage of development in the sixteenth century. Until the end of the century only England, Sweden and northern Germany were successfully manufacturing cast-iron ordnance, and the examples from the *Grifón* presumably came from the latter region. The quality of these castings is excellent and, unlike the Lisbon-manufactured *media culebrina*, their bores run absolutely true.

27 Bronze guns from *El Gran Grifón*: top, the *media culebrina*, sectioned to show its off-centre bore; bottom, the *media sacre* (see back cover).

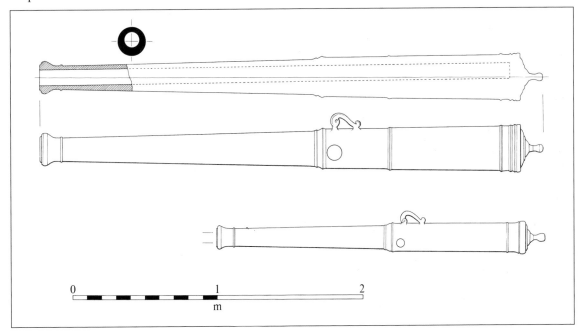

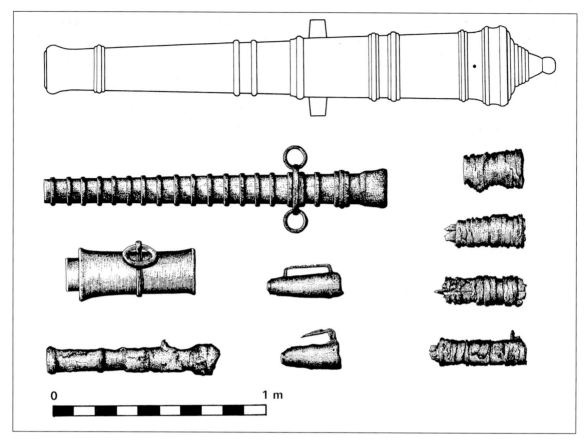

28 Iron artillery from *El Gran Grifón*, probably of German origin: top, a cast-iron 6-pounder; bottom, barrels and breech-blocks from wrought iron breech-loading pieces.

29 Impacted lead balls of musket and arquebus calibre (approx. 12 and 20 mm). These are almost certainly English projectiles fired into the ship during the Armada battles.

Altogether the wreck yielded 4594 pieces of lead shot for the firearms carried by the soldiers on board. It might be thought that such mundane and simple objects would not merit individual study. But careful examination has revealed that a dozen or so balls bear evidence of high-velocity impact – in other words, they had been fired into the ship at close range (**29**). They are presumably English projectiles discharged in the heat of the 1588 battles, and are perhaps the most immediate and evocative mementoes of that historic conflict that an Armada shipwreck could have produced.

3
'In the sight of our men att land' – the *Swan*, 1653

Colonel Cobbett's expedition

In September 1653 a Commonwealth flotilla entered the Sound of Mull off the west coast of Scotland. Its objective was to capture Duart Castle, the ancient seat of Clan Maclean, whose chieftains had held it since before the mid fourteenth century (30). The castle, set on a rocky headland overlooking the narrows which separate Mull from the mainland at Morvern, dominates both the Sound and the entrance to Loch Linnhe, at the head of which lie the western gateways into the Highlands through Lochaber and Glencoe. This vulnerable back-door into Britain was barred a year later by a

30 Duart Castle on Mull, seat of the Maclean clan. The wreck of the *Swan* lies just off the headland on the extreme right.

Cromwellian stronghold at Inverlochy, and in 1690 by Fort William, but in 1653 London's concerns about possible Dutch designs on this unguarded route were given added urgency by a local Royalist revolt.

Scotland's situation at the close of the Civil War was complex and confused. Following the execution of Charles I in 1649 and the establishment of republican government in Britain, Oliver Cromwell had embarked on a brutal subjugation of Ireland. In June 1650 the exiled Charles II, after signing a covenant which repudiated his father's religious policies, landed in Scotland. Cromwell responded by marching north with his New Model Army and, at Dunbar on 4 September 1650, inflicted a crushing defeat on a larger force of Scottish Royalists under General David Leslie.

Notwithstanding this, Charles was crowned King of Scots at Scone on 1 January 1651. Cromwell's response was delayed by illness, but in July his army crossed the Forth and annihilated the Royalist forces at Inverkeithing on 20 July before marching through Fife to capture Perth.

In a desperate counter-measure Charles led his depleted army into England where, on 3 September, he was decisively defeated at Worcester. After narrowly avoiding capture he fled back into exile on the Continent. Scotland was now placed under firm military control, with major strongholds at Ayr, Perth and Leith, and 20 smaller garrisons gripping the rest of the country, including the Highlands.

Royalist revolt, however, continued through 1653 and into 1654 with a rising in the west led by the Earl of Glencairn. Among his supporters were the Macleans of Duart whose chief, Sir Hector, had been killed at Inverkeithing along with several hundred of his clan. Although the revolt was sporadic and ill-organized, Cromwell was determined to nip it in the bud, and dispatched a task-force to the Western Isles. Three vessels, carrying provisions, munitions, siege equipment and about 1000 troops, sailed from Leith via Orkney and Lewis, where the garrisons were reinforced and new fortifications begun. The fleet then proceeded to Dunstaffnage (near Oban), where contact was made with three vessels from the base at Ayr, including a small warship, the *Swan*.

The combined force of six ships, under the command of Colonel Ralph Cobbett, then launched its attack on Mull. Cobbett was a hard-line New Model Army officer who, five years earlier, had commanded the detachment which brought Charles I from captivity at Carisbrooke to face his trial. The outraged Charles had been manhandled into a waiting coach by Cobbett, who had added insult to injury by refusing to remove his hat in the presence of the King.

When Cobbett's expedition anchored in Duart Bay and landed troops and siege artillery on the headland below the castle, no resistance was encountered. The Maclean chief, Sir Allan, who was only nine, had wisely decamped with his household and the Earl of Glencairn to the neighbouring island of Tiree. Seizing his opportunity, the Macleans' hereditary enemy, the Marquis of Argyll, came to Duart to assist Cobbett in rounding up members of the clan and coercing them into submission. Thus far the operation had been an outstanding success, achieved without firing a shot.

What happened next is recorded in a letter sent to Cromwell by Robert Lilburne, the senior Commonwealth commander in Scotland, from Leith on 22 September:

> While our men staid on this Island the 13th instant there hapned a most violent storme, which continued for 16 or 18 houres together, in which wee lost a small Man of Warre called the Swan that came from Aire, the Martha and Margrett of Ipswich, wherein was all our remayning stores of ammunition and provision, only the great Guns and Morterpeeces were saved. But that which was most sad was the loss of the Speedwell of Lyn, where all the men that were in her, being 23 seamen and souldiers (except one) were drowned. The rest of the Men of Warre and others of the fleete were forced to cutt their Masts by the board, and yet hardly escaped: wee lost alsoe 2 of our shallops; and all this in the sight of our Men att land, who saw their freinds drowning, and heard them crying for helpe, but could not save them [**colour plate 4**].

At a stroke Cobbett had lost his entire fleet: three ships sunk and the remaining three dismasted and disabled. The surviving vessels were sent south for repair while Cobbett and his men, with the help of Argyll and in considerable peril of their lives ('the poor men have a very sad time of it, the storms continuing daily very violent'), escaped to Dunstaffnage in small boats and then made their way overland to Dumbarton.

The captain of the *Swan*, Edward Tarleton, survived his ship's wrecking and in due course obtained the command of the 22-gun *Islip*. He was not a fortunate officer. Two years later the *Islip* was herself lost in mysterious circumstances somewhere off western Scotland.

The wreck off Duart Point

In February 1979 John Dadd, a naval diving instructor whose duties had brought him to Mull, discovered a number of iron guns and an anchor scattered on the seabed at the foot of the steep rock face which slopes down from Duart Point. Two lay on a mound of stones which he

31 The seventeenth-century 'Bellarmine' flagon, made at Frechen in the Rhineland, recovered by John Dadd in 1979. Height 21 cm (8_ in).

32 The Archaeological Diving Unit with their research vessel *Xanadu* visiting the site in 1991.

correctly interpreted as ballast from a wreck. A second mound lay a few metres to the west. Further search revealed a number of partially buried artefacts, including a copper cauldron, a badly damaged pewter flagon, and a well-preserved stoneware jar from the Rhineland. The latter dated to around the middle of the seventeenth century (**31**).

For 12 years John Dadd kept the find to himself, hoping one day to return and investigate the wreck more thoroughly. But he never managed to do so and in 1991, anxious that his discovery should be protected from possible depredation, he reported it to the Archaeological Diving Unit (ADU). This government-supported team is based at St Andrews University as part of the Scottish Institute of Maritime Studies, and helps to implement the legislation which allows historic shipwrecks to be protected. A visit to Duart was made that summer, and in due course the wreck was designated by Historic Scotland as a protected archaeological site (**32**).

Before the designation came into effect, however, the wreck was independently discovered by members of the Dumfries and Galloway branch of the Scottish Sub-Aqua Club. When they came upon it during a training dive early in the summer of 1992 they discovered a number of exposed and partially buried items which they recovered and brought ashore. These included a piece of carved wooden decoration in the form of a classical warrior's head (**33**), a corroded mass of silver coins, a grindstone, various wooden objects and the brass lock-plate of a snaphaunce pistol. On being informed of the wreck's prior discovery and its imminent designation, the club members, with commendable public spirit, turned over their finds to the National Museums of Scotland.

On examination in the laboratory the mass of coins was found to bear traces of the cloth bag

33 A carving, depicting a classical warrior's head, recovered during the rescue operations of 1992 (46 x 32 cm).

which had once contained them, impressed in the corroded surface. The metal was too far gone to allow the individual coins to be disassembled, but a few loose ones bore late sixteenth-century dates, so they were evidently quite old when the ship went down. A date much closer to the wrecking, however, was provided by the snaphaunce pistol lock-plate, ornately covered with scrolls and thistles, and of characteristically Scottish shape. The initials G T identify it as coming from the workshop of

George Thomson, an Edinburgh gunsmith who flourished between 1639 and 1661 (34).

A further visit by the ADU revealed that the site was now extensively destabilized, with many vulnerable items emerging from the encapsulating silts along the base of the cliff. Once exposed, these fragile objects, especially those of wood or other organic materials, are prone to mechanical and biological attack, while

34 A lock-plate from a left-handed Scottish snaphaunce pistol with the maker's initials 'G T' – probably George Thomson of Edinburgh (fl. 1639–1661). Length 17.5 cm (7 in).

wreck's mid seventeenth-century date and English origin. Much more exotic, however, were two objects which on first glance seemed to be little more than amorphous lumps of corrosion. Both were X-rayed by industrial radiography in the museum laboratory. The first proved to be an almost intact pocket watch, its brass mechanism miraculously preserved within an outer shell of corrosion (**35**). The second was the hilt of a high-quality rapier, complete with the upper part of its narrow blade and the remains of its leather scabbard. It must have belonged to a senior officer (**36**).

Careful disassembly of the concretion has successfully extracted the rapier's ornate hilt,

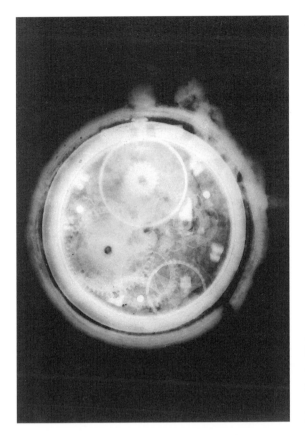

35 Radiograph of a pocket watch, showing its almost intact mechanism.

the fierce currents which sweep across Duart Point during the ebb tide would soon displace them and carry them away. Immediate action was called for if this unique find was not to be degraded or lost.

A crisis response by Historic Scotland provided the resources for a week-long rescue operation by the ADU, supported by students and staff from St Andrews University (**colour plate 5**). Further help was given by the Scottish Sub-Aqua Club, and staff from the National Museums were in attendance throughout. In all, 83 items were recovered and removed to Edinburgh for conservation.

This small sample, although only a tiny proportion of what must still lie buried on the site, gives a remarkable insight to the richness of the wreck and its contents. Clay tobacco pipes, by their characteristic shapes, confirm the

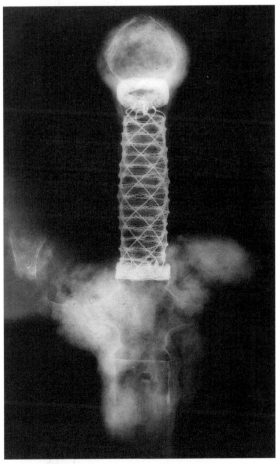

36 Radiograph of a sword, revealing its elaborate hilt. The ferrous elements of the blade and hand-guard have survived only as impressions within the surrounding matrix of concretion.

37 The sword hilt, ornately wound with gold and silver wire, after extraction in the conservation laboratory of the National Museums of Scotland. Length 8.5 cm (3_ in).

wound with gold and silver wire (**37**). Though all the steel of the blade, tang and handguard has corroded to nothing, a negative impression of these parts is preserved in the concretion, and has been recorded carefully during the dismantling of the find. Even the decorative human faces which embellished the guard have been preserved in 'ghost' form (**38**). From this evidence the sword's original appearance can be reconstructed (**39**).

Most excitingly, the oxygen-free environment of the encapsulating silts has preserved organic materials – wood, leather, bone, rope and even textiles – in almost pristine condition. Among the finds was a barrel costrel – a small stave-built vessel which would have been carried as a water-bottle, or perhaps a spirit flask. The master-stave, which incorporates the neck and stopper of the vessel, had been fashioned from solid, with the required curve worked rigidly from the parent wood. In this way the cooper had ensured that the other more flexible staves would bend sweetly to the master-stave when drawn together by the pull of the hoops. Details such as these bring us close to the high levels of skill and sympathetic understanding of materials which seventeenth-century craftsmen brought to their everyday tasks (**40**).

Although cooper-built containers were in wide contemporary use, turned vessels were common too. Finds from the Duart wreck include a lathe-turned pedestal cup and a fine bowl, with tool marks still crisp on their surfaces.

Of all the organic objects, the most unexpected were pieces of the ship's carved decoration. To the helmeted classical head found by the Dumfries and Galloway divers the ADU recovery operation added a winged cherub, a long scrolled carving, and the lower part of a device incorporating a coronet, three ostrich feathers and the motto 'ICH DIEN'. This

badge, often incorrectly identified as that of the Prince of Wales, in fact belongs to the Heir Apparent to the English throne (**41**). Its discovery identifies the wreck as almost certainly that of the *Swan*.

38 A decorative human head on the sword's hand-guard surviving as an impression within the concretion. Traces of gilding can be seen, particularly in the nostrils and mouth.

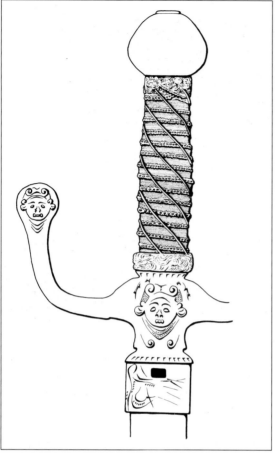

39 A reconstruction of the sword, based on surviving components and concretion impressions.

The King's new pinnace

Robert Lilburne's account of the Duart incident notes the names of the three ships which were lost: the *Martha and Margaret* of Ipswich, the *Speedwell* of Lynn and a small warship called the *Swan*. Both the former were merchant ships which had been employed in transporting supplies from East Anglia to Cromwell's forces in Scotland, and were requisitioned as troop transports for the expedition to Mull. The *Speedwell* also carried the train of siege guns and mortars earmarked for the reduction of Duart Castle. The *Swan*, however, was a one-time royal ship, and of the three only she could have carried the personal emblem of the King's heir on her decorated stern. This conclusion was later reinforced by the discovery of carvings

depicting the emblems of Scotland and Ireland, countries over which Charles I had held dominion.

The *Swan's* origins go back to the early years of Charles' reign, when the lumbering high-charged galleons he had inherited from his father's navy proved incapable of protecting shipping in the English Channel against the

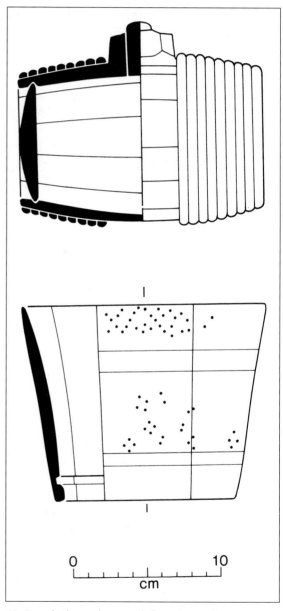

40 Stave-built wooden utensils from the wreck: top, a barrel costrel; bottom, a small flared bucket with punched decoration.

depredations of Turkish and North African pirates and, particularly, Dutch and Flemish privateers whose ships were built to a revolutionary new design. These nimble vessels had been developed at Dunkirk, the main privateering base. They could run rings round a front-line warship, noted a contemporary observer, because the latter was like a giant, 'strong and invincible at a close and grappling, but for all that so weak and impotent in his legs that any active and nimble dwarf, keeping out of reach, may affront and scorn him'.

The Dunkirkers were indeed nimble dwarfs. Variously described as 'pinnaces' and 'frigates' (terms which were to change in meaning over the years), these ships were long and lightly-built, characteristics which gave a fast performance at the cost of a short working life. With oars as well as sails to give added mobility and independence of the wind they were ideal vessels for piracy, and the stream of merchant ships which plied the English Channel and its approaches provided rich pickings.

Many of the victims were English. Though there were some attempts towards the end of James VI and I's reign to build similar ships as a

41 Carvings associated with the Stewart monarchy: top, the lower part of the Heir Apparent's badge, with its 'Ich Dien' motto; bottom, the national symbols of Ireland and Scotland.

counter-measure, these were failures, apparently because English shipwrights insisted on beefing-up their slender construction, so negating the very characteristics which imparted high performance. In 1628 ten purpose-built vessels which could be rowed as well as sailed – the *Lion's Whelps* – entered Charles I's service and achieved some success. They were modelled on the fast continental pinnaces, and displaced around 170 tons. But they were not suited to bad weather, and depredations to English shipping in the Channel continued.

In 1635 a Flushing frigate built on the lines of a Dunkirker fell into English hands. She was single-decked, equipped with oars, and went 'like a sprite' according to a contemporary observer. Her name was the *Swan* (though this ship is not, as will shortly be explained, the one which lies off Duart Point). The ship was taken into the navy, and the King ordered his master-shipwright, Phineas Pett, to construct two frigates along similar lines. These, the *Greyhound* and the *Roebuck*, were duly built, but again the propensity of conservative English shipwrights to add strength and weight prevailed and they did not live up to expectations. The 120-ton *Roebuck* was later described as 'not a good goer', although she was 'strong and able to indure any sea'.

The lack of fast frigates to engage in anti-piracy operations was of particular concern in Ireland, whose waters were infested with corsairs from as far afield as Algiers. Accordingly, Thomas Wentworth, Ireland's Lord Deputy, acquired on his own initiative a 160-ton Dutch-built pinnace, the *Confidence*, in 1637. Described as 'an extraordinarily good sailer', she gave excellent service until 1641 when her owner, now the Earl of Strafford, was impeached for treason by the Long Parliament and beheaded. As the late Earl's private property the ship was then sold, but the King ordered the building of a replica to replace her. This new ship was to be called the *Swan*.

On 8 July 1641 a warrant noted that 'the king is pleased that his new pinnace, the *Swan*, now in Ireland shall be employed this year for the guard of the Irish Seas.' Under the command of John Bartlett the ship was soon active in the confused preliminaries to the Civil War, plying between the Welsh ports, Chester and Ireland in support of the King's forces on the mainland and the Irish Royalists under the Duke of Ormonde. In March 1642 she sailed from Milford Haven to Duncannon in County Wexford (capturing a French ship on the way) to evacuate Protestant settlers who were being attacked by Catholic Irish rebels. By the end of the month she was at Waterford rescuing more Protestant refugees, including the Countess of Ormonde, and transporting them to safety in Dublin.

During 1643 and 1644 the *Swan* provided a vital link between Royalist enclaves in Ireland and North Wales, running the blockade of an increasingly strong and aggressive Parliamentary navy. Her capture, when it came in November

1645, was unexpected and ignominious. Captain Bartlett had anchored off Dublin and gone ashore, where he remained in a state of embarrassment because 'he had no money to pay his sailors'. At this point the Parliamentary vessel *Josline*, commanded by Captain Clarke, hove alongside. By the simple expedient of offering regular pay Clarke persuaded the *Swan's* disgruntled crew to change sides.

Shortly afterwards Clarke took command of the *Swan*, and she fought in the Parliamentary cause against Royalist and pirate shipping in the Irish Sea and off the west coast of Scotland. By 1653 the ship had been assigned to Cromwell's new naval base at Ayr, under Captain Edward Tarleton. From there she sailed for Mull to join Colonel Cobbett's task-force.

The mystery of the carvings

Although there can be little doubt that the remains off Duart Point are those of the *Swan*, the discovery on her wreck of carvings associated with the Stewart monarchy – particularly the badge of the Heir Apparent – is surprising. Such overt Royalist symbolism would have been deeply offensive to republican sentiment. So sensitive were the Parliamentarians to the very concept of kingship that, on the morning of Charles I's execution, an Act was passed against the proclamation of any successor to him. This ensured, in their eyes at any rate, that the crown would not pass automatically to his exiled son the moment the King's head fell from his shoulders. Why then did such hated and potent symbols of royal authority remain with the vessel after she had become a Commonwealth warship?

A possible explanation can be advanced. When the Commonwealth was established in 1649, kingship had been declared 'unnecessary, burdensome, and dangerous to the liberty, safety, and public interest of the people', and the royal arms were ordered to be removed from all public places, particularly churches. Many were destroyed or defaced, but some were hidden, or turned around so that the Commonwealth's arms could be painted on the back. Following the restoration of Charles II, a statute was issued demanding the removal of all Commonwealth symbols, and their replacement with the royal arms. This resulted in many of the old arms being brought out of hiding and re-erected in the locations from which they had been removed.

That this may also have happened aboard the King's former ships is indicated by Samuel Pepys, whose diary entry for 11 May 1660 records that 'this morning we began to pull down all the State's arms in the fleet, having first sent to Dover for painters and others to come to set up the King's.' The possibility that the *Swan* had removed but not discarded her royal emblems is reinforced by two archaeological observations.

First, while the Duart carvings have nail-holes for attachment to the outside of the hull, no trace of the fixings themselves has survived. It seems likely therefore that the carvings were not in their original locations when the ship was lost. The very survival of such features – these are the first finds of their kind ever to be made on a wreck in British waters – further suggests that they may not have been in their original vulnerable locations on the upper and outer parts of the hull at the time of wrecking, but stowed safely below. Perhaps their retention was a tacit recognition that things can change in politics, or perhaps they had been preserved as trophies. We will probably never know.

Rescuing the *Swan*

By the summer of 1992 it was clear that the shipwreck off Duart Point represented a major and quite unprecedented part of Scotland's heritage. Significant remains of the vessel apparently survived beneath piles of her own ballast, while the surrounding sediments encapsulated rich deposits of well-preserved archaeological material. The wreck was likely to be a rich repository of first-hand evidence about contemporary nautical technology, warfare and everyday life at sea. And, since the *Swan's* career

included service with both sides in the Civil War, her remains represented a unique microcosm of the great historical events in which she had played a part. It was imperative that the wreck should be protected and, if necessary, its contents rescued and preserved.

The responsibility for dealing with ancient shipwrecks in Scottish waters had, at the time, only recently passed from the Department of National Heritage in London to Historic Scotland, and the *Swan* (described somewhat prosaically as 'Designation no. 3 (Scotland), 1992') was duly declared a protected historic wreck by the Secretary of State. This secured the site against human depredation, for unlicensed diving on it now became a criminal offence, but it could do nothing to mitigate the greater threat of environmental damage. Something was triggering heavy erosion of the sediments piled up against the foot of the cliff, and this erosion showed no signs of stopping.

Graphic indications of these destructive processes at work had already been recorded by the ADU. A carved wooden cherub, for example, was found in a partly uncovered state, one wing still securely buried while the face and opposite wing were exposed (**42**). Barnacles had begun to colonize the unprotected surface of the wood. The density of their distribution increased towards the upper edge of the exposed wing, where the oldest animals were clustered. None of these, however, was aged more than six months.

Shortly before that time the cherub must have been completely buried. Its progressive exposure to a point at which more than half had been revealed is chronicled by the barnacle infestation. Had the process been allowed to continue the whole object would, in a relatively short time, have become completely uncovered, and in addition to damage caused by the barnacles (they embed themselves deeply into the surface of the wood), further biological decay would have set in, exacerbated by the abrasive effect of the moving sediments. In any event, the object, once freed from encapsulation,

42 Organic material exposed by shifting sediments, photographed by the Archaeological Diving Unit in 1992. In the foreground is a staved wooden vessel; above it a human arm-bone. Scale in centimetres.

would quickly have been carried away by the strong ebb tide.

Another item was rescued as it was on the point of being borne away by currents. This was the major part of a hand-built Hebridean *crogan* pot, no doubt a container for some commodity acquired locally by the ship (43). A circle of barnacle infestation on its outer side indicated that, until recently, only a small part of it had been exposed. On this secure gritty surface a kelp plant had established itself and begun to prosper. When the sediments shifted to leave the *crogan* loose on the seabed the drag of current on the kelp plant's fronds began to pull the pot and its unwitting passenger with the tide. Both were found some distance from the site and rescued before they could move further.

Countless thousands of infinitely varied processes, interacting with one another and with the environmental inputs of water movement, shifting sediments, and chemical and biological activity in a web of unfathomable complexity, determine the survival, distribution and stability of archaeological material on such a site. A shipwreck is a cataclysmic event both for the human beings involved in the disaster and for the seabed environment within which it takes place. The ordered entity which a ship represents begins an irreversible progression of disordering from the moment of wrecking as various environmental inputs take effect. The seabed upon which the ship has impacted will, at the same time, receive a destabilizing anomaly which is likely to trigger a wide range of responses as the disrupted environment adjusts itself to regain the state of balance towards which nature invariably trends.

In a simplistic sense it is the wreck and not its environment that are of consequence to the archaeologist, who is primarily interested in the ship and its contents as material expressions of the human past. But unless he or she takes account of the environment within which the archaeological manifestations lie, and seeks to understand the mechanisms of destruction, dispersal, integration and stabilization with which the relevant area of sea floor has reacted to the intrusion of the wreck, he or she will be unable to interpret the observed remains in archaeological terms. It will be impossible to work backwards, as it were, through the wrecking process, and so draw conclusions about the ship before it became a wreck.

By the autumn of 1992 it was obvious that various destructive forces had been affecting the Duart Point wreck, though the causes were far from clear and their possible effects uncertain. Accordingly, Historic Scotland funded a series of monitoring visits to check whether the erosion was continuing and, if so, to take steps to control it. These visits were carried out over the winter of 1992–3 by the Scottish Institute of Maritime Studies from St Andrews University, supported by members of the Dumfries and Galloway Sub-Aqua Club.

It was fortunate that the visits were made, for erosion was continuing apace. On one occasion a complex of organic material was revealed, including a shoe, rope, a barrel stave, a wooden pulley and several fragmentary objects. These were temporarily protected by spreading fresh gravel over them. On another visit shifting sediments had revealed an almost intact wooden bowl, and two carvings which bore the emblems of Scotland and Ireland. In this instance the finds were recovered and delivered to Edinburgh for conservation.

Despite these initial successes, the long-term future of the wreck was uncertain. Historic Scotland, though keen to protect and manage the site, had neither the resources nor the diving expertise necessary for positive intervention. The National Museums of Scotland were eager to acquire, conserve and ultimately display the wreck material, but their budgets were already over-stretched and wreck collections, because of their richness and variety, are expensive to deal with, and especially to conserve. Finally, the ADU, which had done so much to help resolve the original crisis, was responsible for the monitoring of all designated historic wrecks off Britain, and could not devote further time to a single site, however important it might be.

Further work on the site demanded a dedicated long-term project which brought together a team of experienced underwater archaeologists, adequately financed and equipped. The nucleus of such a team already existed in the Scottish Institute of Maritime Studies and, after a successful fund-raising campaign, the project was launched. Its patron is Sir Lachlan Maclean of Duart, against whose ancestors Cobbett's fleet had sailed and whose castle is once again the centre of his clan.

43 Hebridean *crogan* pot showing evidence of recent exposure (the area of barnacle colonization) and subsequent transport down-current under the drag of a kelp plant.

44 A general plan of the wreck site.

At the time of writing, five six-week field seasons have been conducted on the wreck, and a full survey and site assessment has been carried out. A programme of consolidation has stabilized the erosion, at least in the short term, and limited excavation has begun. The site's richness has been confirmed beyond all expectations, and over the next few years it is hoped that a carefully controlled rescue excavation will preserve for posterity the unique material now under threat.

Anatomy of a wreck site

As a result of five years' detailed investigation much more is now understood of the site and its dynamics. The information upon which this understanding is based was obtained, as with all archaeological work, by slow and painstaking observation and recording. Most of the survey techniques are identical to those employed on land. A baseline is established, and rigid grids are used to provide accurate reference for drawing frames which allow every square metre to be mapped at a scale of 1:10.

Each item with a dimension of 5 cm or more, including all natural features, was recorded on the plan (**44**). Systematic vertical photography added further detail (**45**). Contours were plotted at 10-cm intervals to reveal the subtleties of the underwater topography, and scientific instruments used to obtain data about the speed

45 A diving archaeologist taking vertical photographs of the ship's structural remains. Note the triangular 'targets' used to rectify the photographs within the overall site grid.

and direction of currents. An inventory was made of the flora and fauna which inhabited the site, and their possible effects assessed. For example, by plotting the distributions of kelp species, information was obtained about the site's micro-environments. One sub-type indicates high-energy environments, another does best in low-energy areas, while a third species exploits the intermediate zones.

Further evidence about the environmental characteristics of different parts of the site has been obtained by a careful examination of the way in which large iron objects – particularly cannons – have undergone chemical change. Oxygenated seawater, especially when it is in a constant state of movement, has a strong corrosive effect on iron. The products of this corrosion act as a binding cement which, in due course, builds a concretion of sand, shells and sometimes even adjacent small artefacts, around the decaying iron object. This affords it a measure of protection although, within the concretion, the surviving ferrous residues become increasingly degraded and unstable.

By recording the thickness and composition of the concretion, and measuring attributes such as the voltage potential and acidity of the surviving metal, it is possible to reconstruct the environmental changes which have occurred through time. It can be determined, for instance, whether a cannon has been completely exposed since its initial deposition, whether it has been buried until recently, or whether it has been subject to cyclical episodes of exposure and reburial. Examples of all three such histories are evident on the cannons examined on the Duart Point wreck, and this information adds to our understanding of the processes which have been operating over the site as a whole.

It is now possible to suggest, albeit tentatively, the sequence of the *Swan's* wrecking and subsequent deposition. The ship probably hit Duart Point broadside on, with her bow pointing towards the west. She would have been forced hard against the shore by the 'violent storme' (almost certainly a strong north-

westerly gale), grounding among the waves crashing over the rocks. In such weather, and in an age when few could swim, the deceptively narrow gap was too wide for those on board to cross, and those on shore could do little to help them.

The lower part of the hull would have pounded against the jagged rock face, staving in the bilges and engulfing the hold with water. Drawn by the weight of ballast and back-tow from the breaking waves, the disintegrating ship would then have lurched and bumped sideways down the rock face to land at its foot, some 10 m (32 ft) down. Most of her masts and spars, if not torn away earlier, would still have protruded above water. Loose parts of the ship, and other floating objects (including bodies) would have detached themselves from the wreck, either to be cast ashore or borne away by the currents.

Although the hull itself probably remained at least partially intact, its interior would have been in a state of chaos. Objects heavier than water would have tumbled downwards until prevented from moving further by parts of the ship, or the sea floor. Larger objects, such as guns, may have caused considerable damage as they tore free of their lashings and crashed through the disintegrating ship. Lighter material, on the other hand, would have worked its way upwards until it either floated clear or became trapped against a deck or bulkhead within the hull.

The processes of disintegration and eventual stabilization probably took many years to complete (indeed, as the recent events have shown, full stabilization has never been achieved). During this phase a good deal of material was certainly lost, but much was also preserved. The main agent of preservation appears to have been the strong west–east current which, particularly during rough weather, deposits fresh silt on the site. Eddies carry much of this silt towards the base of the cliff, where the wreck lies. It seems likely that when the hull was at least partly intact these silts accumulated in its interior, encapsulating the debris trapped inside.

Work on the site has now demonstrated that much of the ship's stern, which lies at the eastern end of the site, has in effect collapsed in on itself, entrapping much of the interior structure of the after-cabin together with its contents. A remarkable find in this area was part of the ship's binnacle – a wooden box-like structure with three compartments which once contained two compasses and a lantern, and stood in front of the steersman on the ship's after-deck (46).

The base of a mariner's compass still lay in one of the outer compartments of the binnacle. A matching compass would have been located in the compartment at the other side, while the middle space would have contained a lantern to light the compasses by night. Two compasses were required because the steersman conned the ship by means of a long lever, called a whipstaff, which he moved from one side of the deck to the other. He therefore needed to be able to view a compass from whichever side of the ship he happened to be. To avoid magnetic interference the binnacle is fastened with small oak pegs rather than iron nails, in the manner prescribed by contemporary authorities. The fact that the magnetic influence of each compass would have affected adversely the accuracy of the other does not seem to have occurred to seventeenth-century navigators.

Evidence of a small drama which once befell one of the *Swan's* steersmen is preserved in the remains of the binnacle (47). It appears that, perhaps through inattention, the lantern was allowed to burn a hole through the top of the box. This was subsequently repaired, rather crudely, with a wooden patch, secured, most inappropriately, with iron nails.

46 The remains of the ship's binnacle, or compass housing, exposed during excavation. The base of a compass can be seen in the right-hand compartment. Scale in cm.

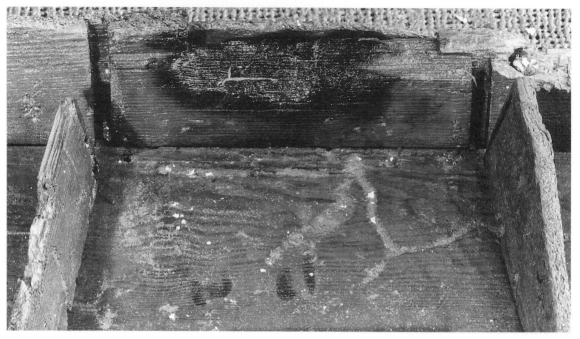

47 A detail of the binnacle's central compartment, showing the scorched hole at the top and its inexpert repair. Four small burn marks can also be seen at bottom centre.

48 A complete compass during excavation. It is upside-down, and its base has been forced inwards by water pressure as the ship sank. Traces of a cloth cover still adhere to its wooden surface. Scale in cm.

1 Tobermory Bay, Isle of Mull. The *San Juan de Sicilia* blew up and sank just off the pier at the right of the harbour front.

2 A diving archaeologist using a drawing grid on the wreck of *El Gran Grifón* off Fair Isle.

3 The broken *media culebrina* from *El Gran Grifón* is hoisted ashore.

4 A reconstruction drawing by Andrew McIlvride of the wrecking of the *Swan* off Duart Point on 13 September 1653.

5 The Archaeological Diving Unit during the rescue
  operation off Duart Point in 1992.

6 The *Dartmouth* bell, recovered in 1973.

7 Part of the *Dartmouth's* surviving structure, revealed during excavation.

8 A navigator's protractor from the *Dartmouth*, made by John Lewis of Dublin.

9 Archaeologist Tony Long extracts a gold coin from the wreckage of the *Dartmouth*.

10 The two gold coins found on the *Dartmouth:* left, a William and Mary guinea of 1689; right, a James II guinea of 1687.

11 Rhenish stoneware 'Bellarmines' from the
   Kennemerland, 1664. Some were used to
   transport mercury.

12 Sealing wax impressions on the backs of playing cards
   showing the obverse and reverse of the mint dies at
   Middelburg used to strike ducatons in 1728.
   This evidence was produced in the Admiralty Court at
   Edinburgh to prove the identity of the *Adelaar's* wreck.

13 Gold jewellery from the *Adelaar*.

14 A diving conservator attaches a sacrificial aluminium anode to one of the heavily corroded cast-iron guns on the Duart Point wreck site as part of a programme of *in situ* conservation.

15 Sandbags protect fragile organic deposits on the Duart Point wreck site.

16 A visitor swims round the underwater heritage trail established on the Duart Point wreck site by Historic Scotland and the Duart Point project. This was the first scheme of its kind to be operated on a designated historic shipwreck in Britain: another has now been established on the nearby *Dartmouth* wreck.

17 The opening of a wreck information board at Duart – another first for Historic Scotland. Represented on site are the various partners in this multi-faceted project – Historic Scotland, the National Museums of Scotland, the University of St Andrews, HM Coastguard, and Sir Lachlan and Lady Maclean of Duart.

Binnacles of this period are exceedingly rare, and this is the first to be found in British waters. This makes the discovery one of considerable importance in its own right, but it is significant for another reason too. A binnacle is a fragile structure, secured only lightly to the upper deck of the vessel. Its survival therefore emphasizes the degree to which the stern parts of the wreck off Duart Point have been preserved.

More recent excavation has confirmed the extent of this preservation. Among the finds is an almost intact compass, complete with the brass gimbals which kept it level against the movement of the ship (**48** and **49**). Close by, excavation revealed a chaotic jumble of debris derived from the structure and contents of a well fitted-out cabin – almost certainly that of the captain, Edward Tarleton. It included beautifully crafted panelling and an elaborate door, more suited to an elegant drawing-room than to the interior of a small warship. Amongst it was a scatter of ship's fittings, domestic items, leather shoes, musket

49 The compass bowl (minus its bottom) after recovery. Its brass gimbal ring would have been attached to an outer box, allowing it to keep level in spite of the ship's movement. A piece of the cloth cover can be seen at the lower left. Diameter 17 cm (6¾ in).

bullets and a 4-pound lead weight on which was stamped the crowned monogram of Charles I, the sword of the City of London and the tiny figure of the Archangel Michael carrying a pair of scales which is the mark of the city's Worshipful Company of Plumbers (**50**). Scattered through these deposits were parts of a disarticulated human skeleton (or perhaps skeletons) (**51**).

These finds suggest that the Duart wreck is the most complete and exciting underwater discovery to be made in Britain since the *Mary Rose*. But, like all good archaeological finds, it poses new questions as well as providing answers to old ones. The most compelling of these concern the ship's lavish embellishment, inside and out. For a vessel intended to out-perform the nimble pirates

50 Control marks on a 4-pound lead weight. Left, the crowned monogram of Charles I; lower centre, the figure of the Archangel Michael with a set of scales, the mark of the Worshipful Company of Plumbers; right, sword mark denoting the City of London.

51 Human bones from the wreck.

of the Channel approaches and the waters around Ireland, these decorative additions seem most inappropriate, since such ships were supposed to combine lightness with flexibility. Every surplus pound, or piece of structure which imparted excessive rigidity, was a liability.

Elaborate decorative carving on the King's ships (especially his smaller ones) was not only an unnecessary expense, as the naval administrator John Hollond railed in 1638, it also represented an unproductive addition to weight. The *Swan's* builders (or perhaps the King himself, for whom royal dignity and symbolic embellishment always took precedence over practicalities) clearly did not agree. Then again, as Nathaniel Butler pointed out about the same time, the widespread practice of panelling cabins in small ships was entirely misplaced, for not only did it add weight but also tended to make 'an offensive cracking and noise whensoever the ship worketh much in a grown sea'. Moreover, its inaccessible spaces provided 'a harbour for rats'. In Butler's view a skilled joiner should never be let near such a ship: an honest workaday carpenter was all that was required.

Why then did the *Swan*, ostensibly built to out-sail the pirate ships on whose design she had been based, incorporate these debilitating non-essentials? Only archaeology could have posed these questions, and only further archaeological evidence can supply the answers. The Duart Point shipwreck will certainly be the focus of much underwater archaeological activity in Scotland for many years to come.

4
The witches' revenge – the *Dartmouth*, 1690

'This miserable melancholy station'

As Captain Edward Pottinger paced the deck of their Majesties' 5th-rate warship *Dartmouth* at anchor in Scallastle Bay off the Isle of Mull on 9 October 1690, he was not a happy man (**52**). His ship was old and in bad repair: on 2 September he had reported that 'no manner of stuff [sheathing and tallow] was left upon her bottome', and that her anchor cables, with frequent deep-water use, were 'soo extremely worn, as not to be trusted'. The carpenter and

boatswain had reported that their stores were depleted to the point of exhaustion, while even the ship's longboat 'with continuall rowing and

52 The Sound of Mull, looking across from Morvern to the island. The *Dartmouth* anchored in Scallastle Bay, towards the upper right of the photograph. During the storm of 9 October 1690 she parted from her anchors and was driven across the Sound to strike the right-hand tip of Eilean Rubha an Ridire (the islet at centre left), where her wreck now lies.

night service [was] soe much shaken as either a new boat or great repair will be wanting'.

A month later his dwindling supplies were on the point of running out. There was not, he had complained on 4 October, 'an ounce of butter aboard, nor pease ... our men being three days without flesh, in less than a fortnight after sailing, and truly our circumstances has been extreame ill.' On top of all this neither he nor his sailors had been paid for several months. The west coast of Scotland was, he had lamented earlier in the summer, a 'miserable melancholy station'.

The *Dartmouth* had departed from Greenock on 14 May 1690 as the flagship of a squadron sent out to ravage the recalcitrant Jacobite clans of the Western Isles and bring them to heel. The operation was part of General Hugh Mackay's campaign to secure allegiance to the new regime of William and Mary by rooting out adherents of the deposed James II, in the wake of the Jacobite army's defeat at Cromdale two weeks earlier. In addition to the *Dartmouth* there were two smaller warships, the 6th-rate *Lark* and the sloop *Fanfan*. Another 6th-rate, the *James Galley*, appears to have served as a dispatch vessel, while the Glasgow frigate the *Lamb* was also attached to Pottinger's fleet. Five hired merchant ships carried a regiment of 900 government troops commanded by Major James Ferguson of the Cameronians. In their holds were tools and materials for the construction of a new fort at Inverlochy.

General Mackay's orders stipulated that the fleet's two senior officers should exercise joint command, with Ferguson taking responsibility for land operations and Pottinger directing matters afloat. Their task was 'to make a diversion, allarme the rebells coasts, cut their communication with the Islanders now in rebellione against their Majesties authoritie, and to take away or burn all their boats and birlins'. Those rebels who gave up their weapons and swore allegiance to William and Mary were to be pardoned and protected, but this dispensation did not apply to their chiefs. Only

by 'casting themselves in the King's mercy and delyvering their persons prisoners to the said major' could the latter atone for their treason, though should they do so Ferguson was 'required to treat them civilly'. The strategem was one of stick and carrot.

Information about the campaign is contained in a number of dispatches sent by Captain Pottinger to the Navy Board, the log of the sloop *Fanfan* (the *Dartmouth's* own log did not survive her wrecking), and in the state papers of England and Scotland. At first things went well. Between 17 and 19 May Gigha, Cara, Colonsay and Jura were raided. Towards the end of May parts of Mull were ravaged, and on 27 May the *Fanfan* 'stood within pistoll shott of Dewart Castle they fired at us with their small shott and we made 3 shott at ye castle and hitt ye upper parts.' The Macleans of Duart were among the most intractable of the rebels, and a night reconnaissance by the *Fanfan's* boats revealed a force of between 500 and 600 hostile clansmen in the vicinity of the castle. Ferguson and Pottinger prudently decided to muster more troops before dealing with them.

Early June saw the task force active around Islay, Rhum, Eigg and Canna, before it descended on Skye on the 7th. Ferguson's troops were put ashore in Ornsay Bay, not far from the Macdonald stronghold at Sleat, while Pottinger's ships cannonaded a large party of clansmen who had come to oppose them. All this was too much for the chief's son, Sir Donald, who by the evening of 8 June was on board the *Dartmouth* signing his oath of allegiance. Pottinger's gunboat diplomacy was taking effect and, in addition to the Macdonalds, the Mackenzies and Macleods were now showing signs of moderating their Jacobite stance.

But it was a fragile stalemate rather than abject surrender. The Macdonald chief, old Sir Donald, was in Ireland gathering support from his kinsmen there, and remained steadfastly opposed to the Williamite regime. Neither did all of his clan accept his son's easy capitulation to Pottinger. Three stragglers from the *Dartmouth* who had tarried while returning to their boats during the invasion of Skye were killed by a group of Macdonalds from Eigg; a fourth, who had managed to hide, was later discovered and lynched. Pottinger's response was uncharacteristically brutal, and later hushed-up by officialdom. His troops descended on Eigg, where only women, children, and the elderly remained, and exacted a savage reprisal of murder and rape.

The theatre of operations now moved back to the southern Hebrides, with further attacks on Islay and Mull. On 20 June the *Fanfan* cruised up the Sound of Mull, firing at armed parties on the shore and, on one occasion, putting out a landing party to engage in a sharp fire-fight in which nine rebels were killed before the survivors fled into the mountains. The following day *Fanfan* was off the Macleans' isolated stronghold at Cairnburgh in the Treshnish Isles, where she fired at clansmen manning the fortifications and noted six boats hauled up on shore.

By the beginning of July the campaign was moving towards its climax. On 3 July General Mackay had reached Inverlochy with 3000 troops, and two days later he began building a fort on top of the earlier Cromwellian citadel (see p. 46) which was to be known thereafter as Fort William. It was constructed in 11 days, and among those conscripted to throw up its earthwork bastions were the 'disgusted seamen' of the *Dartmouth*. The ship was also obliged to surrender six of her guns to arm the fort against a feared attack by the French.

This fear was not misplaced. On 30 June an Anglo-Dutch fleet had been defeated off Beachy Head, and a strike against western Scotland, still aflame with Jacobite sentiment, was an obvious way in which the French might exploit their victory. An attempt was indeed made, but on a small scale. Late in July old Sir Donald Macdonald came back from Ireland in a French frigate, complete with a commission from James VII and II and £1000 with which to start a fresh

revolt. Pottinger and the *Dartmouth* at once hurried to Armadale to nip the situation in the bud.

In response to Sir Donald 'belching out [verbal] defiances to authority' Pottinger 'complimented the same with 30 or 40 shot' delivered against Armadale Castle as the *Dartmouth* raced through the Sound of Sleat on the ebb tide. He returned at slack water and skilfully manoeuvred his ship with anchors set at bow and stern so that his broadsides could be brought to bear on the castle for upwards of two hours. It was razed to the ground. In the meantime the *Lamb* was meting out a similar treatment, rather unsportingly, to the nearby house of Sir Donald's mistress. As for the old chief himself, the *Dartmouth's* 'whistling nine pounders' had sent him 'scampering to the hills'. For good measure the government forces set fire to the ruins, and burnt nine Macdonald birlins (oared galleys) together with a larger vessel.

But the *Dartmouth* was beginning to suffer from the effects of her prolonged service. Some months earlier she had grounded in the Isles of Scilly, damaging her bottom and loosening some of her outer sheathing planks, including a large part of the cladding over the stem-post which was habitually catching the anchor ropes. It was high time, insisted Pottinger, to lay the ship ashore and repair the damage. Accordingly, the *Dartmouth* returned to Greenock on 26 July. After offloading her guns and ballast she was beached for the duration of a single spring tide, and her damaged hull patched up and cleaned as far as time and limited resources would allow. Pottinger also attempted once more – without success – to obtain the mounting arrears of pay due to himself and his men.

On 27 August the *Dartmouth* left Greenock bound again for her 'melancholy station' among the islands. At Fort William the garrison's elderly colonel, John Hill (he had commanded the original Cromwellian fort in 1654), required no naval support from Pottinger, but asked him to sail to Orkney to collect £1000 which had been allocated to the fort. Mindful of his ship's condition Pottinger declined, and instead engaged in a fresh bout of local gunboat diplomacy. Eigg was again visited, and this time submitted, as did old Sir Donald Macdonald of Armadale in Skye. The only remaining problem centred on the Macleans of Duart who, though offering to submit, insisted on retaining their arms. It was a stratagem that fooled nobody, and Pottinger was once again ordered to the Sound of Mull, there to co-operate with the Earl of Argyll and his regiment in a final show-down with the Macleans.

On 9 September the *Dartmouth*, in company with the *Lark* and the *Lamb*, made a precautionary anchorage in Scallastle Bay, some five miles north-west of Duart. A south-westerly gale had been blowing for two days, and seemed set to increase, so Pottinger decided to ride it out in this relatively sheltered anchorage before proceeding to Duart. It was his last act. That night, according to a report published a fortnight later in the *London Gazette*, 'there arose a very violent storm which forced the said frigate from her anchors and drove her upon a rock, where she broke to pieces, and Captain Pottinger the commander and most of the men were drowned.'

The wreck off Eilean Rubha an Ridire

In August 1973 a group of experienced amateur divers from Bristol came to Mull on holiday. Their purpose was to dive on some of the deeper and more difficult wrecks which litter the Sound, but towards the end of their stay they opted for something easier – the *Ballista*, a small West Highland puffer which had been lost earlier that summer while attempting to salvage coal from a wreck which lay close to the small island of Rubha an Ridire. When they arrived at the site, however, they found the *Ballista* lying almost dry against the rocks, and so they set out on an exploratory dive around the island.

Not far from the *Ballista*, in quite shallow water, one of their number discovered a 2.5 m (8 ft) long iron gun lying almost hidden beneath the dense canopy of kelp fronds which fringed the island. Further searches revealed more guns and three anchors spread over a distance of some 30 m (100 ft), extending down a gully which widened seawards from its narrow apex close inshore. Adhering to one of the guns was a large bronze bell. This was recovered to reveal on one side a *pheon*, or broad arrow, which indicated that the divers had found the wreck of an English naval vessel. On the other side were the letters D H, and the date 1678 (**colour plate 6**). In the vicinity of the bell was a spread of bricks and tiles, evidently debris from the ship's galley.

Other finds included cannon balls, some of which also bore the *pheon* mark, and two sheet-lead Roman numerals which were later identified as draught marks from the stem or stern of the ship. In places, partly obscured by drifts of shingle, traces of wooden structure could be seen. Some scraps of pottery, glassware and clay pipes all indicated a late seventeenth-century date.

Although their holiday was nearly over, the group, whose members had no previous archaeological experience, improvised a detailed survey of the wreck. Using plastic washing line marked off with insulating tape at metre intervals they conducted a basic triangulation of the site, plotting the locations of the guns and other features to build up a preliminary plan. At the end of the visit they reported their recoveries to the local Receiver of Wreck, who advised them that the best way to protect the find from interlopers would be to apply for it to be designated under the Protection of Wrecks Act, which had been passed by Parliament earlier that year. This was duly done, and the wreck was among the first in British waters to be protected in this way.

At this stage there was no indication of the wreck's identity but one of the group, John Adnams, began following up the clues they had discovered on the seabed. The ship was clearly naval, and English, while the date on the bell meant that it must have been wrecked some time after 1678. A visit to the Public Record Office soon brought the loss of the *Dartmouth* in 1690 to light, and the identification was clinched by the letters D H on the bell.

By now the divers, who had formed themselves into the Bristol Undersea Archaeology Group, were keen to investigate the find more fully. From the outset they were determined that the project should be conducted to good archaeological standards, and that the recoveries should be deposited in an appropriate museum. They made contact with St Andrews University, where the Scottish Institute of Maritime Studies had been established that year. The Institute agreed to provide a team of diving archaeologists and the necessary equipment. Next they won the support of the National Museum of Antiquities of Scotland, which offered to sponsor the project and provide conservation facilities. Over the next three years a major part of the wreck site was excavated with outstandingly valuable results, for the *Dartmouth* and her broken remains had some extraordinary stories to tell.

A window into Pepys's navy

The *Dartmouth* was an unusually old ship, and her long life spanned a period of considerable importance in the development of Britain's navy. Built under Cromwell's Commonwealth in 1655, she was named after the Parliamentary general Lord Dartmouth. The ship was constructed in the Portsmouth yards by Sir John Tippets as a 5th-rate frigate. This categorization referred to the captain's rate of pay, which related to the size of his ship. There were six rates in all, so the *Dartmouth* was in the second lowest rated group. She had a keel length of 80 feet (24.4 m), a beam of 25 feet (7.6 m), a laden draught of 12 feet (3.66 m) and a tonnage of 266.

Her armament varied from time to time, and is most fully recorded in the Ordnance Office establishment of 1687, which assigns her 16 9-pounders, 16 6-pounders and 4 3-pounders. She also carried two brass blunderbusses for close-quarter fighting.

Sir John Tippets, who became Surveyor of the Navy in 1672, had studied ship design and construction in Denmark as a young man during the reign of Charles I. In the 1640s radical developments had been taking place in the design of small British warships (see Chapter 3), and in 1646 the first of the so-called 'frigates', the *Constant Warwick*, was built in Pett's yard at Ratcliffe. The hull form of the *Constant Warwick*, according to Samuel Pepys, was 'taken from the Dunkirk frigates, which outsailed all other ships in the seas; and from thence came that improvement. Upon which foundation our frigates from the third rate downwards were built'.

Tippets – who was to rebuild the *Constant Warwick* in 1666 – thus learned his trade as a shipwright against a background of and in intimate contact with a new concept which produced manoeuvrable and fast vessels by combining lightness with fine underwater lines. We may suppose that these influences were strong in his mind when, less than a decade after the *Constant Warwick* had been launched, he laid down the *Dartmouth*'s keel.

The ship's long service in many parts of the world, often involving operations in confined and difficult waters, further points to her excellent sailing qualities. She played a minor role in several engagements with the Dutch, and undertook anti-piracy work not only in British waters but also in the Mediterranean and Caribbean. In April 1666, in company with two other ships, she captured three Dutch merchantmen off the Irish coast, and a few days later assisted in the destruction of a Flushing privateer. In January 1673 the *Dartmouth* recaptured the *Susanna* of Weymouth, which had been taken as a prize, and brought her safely into Plymouth with her cargo of oranges and lemons intact. Later that month she chased two 'capers' – small pirate vessels – and captured one of them.

The next month found her escorting a convoy of merchant ships to Spain, after which she spent the rest of the year patrolling the Irish Sea and ferrying various naval dignitaries including the Duke of Ormonde, one of the Lords of the

Admiralty. Much of 1675 was spent on the Mediterranean station, participating in a campaign against Tripolitanian corsairs and ranging as far as Sicily and the Levant. In 1678 she was sent to Sheerness for a major refit, which included the replacement of her entire keel and the three strakes on either side of it. It was probably at this time that Van de Velde the Younger sketched the ship (**53**).

The refurbished *Dartmouth* was then ordered to take part in Sir John Berry's expedition to put down a rising in Virginia under Nathaniel Bacon. By the time the ship reached America the trouble was largely over, and she sailed for home on 30 April 1677. Little more is heard of her until April 1686, when the Spanish garrison at Puerto Rico (Spain then being an ostensibly friendly power) attempted to prevent the ship from leaving harbour. What followed gave rise to a lengthy piece of doggerel penned by one of her officers, Hovenden Walker, who later became a Rear-Admiral. A few lines from its opening and closing stanzas will suffice:

When the 'Dartmouth' frigot lay off the town
That's called Porto Rico, of some renown
The captain sent thither to know if he cou'd
Come peacably in for water and wood ...

and

Thus fireing, and fireing, we held a good space,
And gave 'em the go by to their disgrace
Three hours or more continu'd the fight,
With fire and smoke, and a very calm night
And tho' within pistol shot we were
Yet nevertheless we got well clear
Without much hurt or any fear
And to tell you the tale we are now come here.

The ship's greatest moments came in the naval war which followed the dynastic settlement of 1688. She was present off Orford Ness when the first reports of the Prince of Orange's expedition to Torbay were received, and took part in the action off Bantry Bay on 1 May 1689 at which, after an indecisive action, the French fleet retired to Brest. Following this she was dispatched to Liverpool to convoy victuallers and transports for the relief of Londonderry, where William of Orange's supporters were holding out against those of King James. On 28 July, under the

53 A sketch by Willem Van de Velde the Younger of a 5th-rate, thought to be the Dartmouth.

command of John Leake and in company with the victuallers *Mountjoy* and *Phoenix*, she broke the defensive boom across the River Foyle and, after a heavy exchange of fire with the shore batteries, enabled the relief ships to get through. A month later she helped to convey the Duke of Schomberg's expedition to the Jacobite-held castle of Carrickfergus, which submitted after a four-day siege. Then the *Dartmouth* joined Commodore Rooke to cruise off Kinsale and Cork before eventually returning to the Downs, where Captain Leake was paid off.

In February 1690 the *Dartmouth* and her new captain, Edward Pottinger, sailed northwards to the 'miserable melancholy station' from which neither would return.

The *Dartmouth*'s remains

During three seasons of excavation much of the *Dartmouth*'s surviving hull was uncovered, and parts of it brought to the surface for conservation and detailed examination. At the same time the surrounding seabed deposits were investigated to determine their environmental relationship with the remains of the wreck, and help to explain the processes whereby the observed archaeological distributions had come about (54).

At first sight the surviving portion of articulated hull structure, measuring some 12 by 4 m (40 x 13 ft) at its maximum extent, did not look a promising basis for reconstructing the hull shape and construction in overall terms. Even at an optimistic estimate it represented no more than about 10 per cent of the ship as a whole. Moreover, it included neither extremity, so there was no indication of where it should be placed on the longitudinal axis of the hull. Nor was it clear which end pointed towards the bow, and which to the stern. Finally, the upper surfaces of the exposed timbers had been heavily abraded by the shallow layer of shingle which lay above them, and which moved freely in storms.

A solution to the orientation of the vessel was obtained through a detailed examination of the finds. Even though the many hundreds of small objects recovered during the excavation appeared, at first sight, to be scattered at random across the site, this was not the case. Different categories of object showed distinctive patterns in their distribution. For example, navigational instruments – a log slate (55), dividers, a protractor (**colour plate 8**), part of a backstaff and a gimballed hanging lamp from the ship's binnacle – were all clustered towards the inshore end of the site. Navigation was, of course, the prerogative of the captain and his officers, who lived and worked at the after- end of the ship.

Objects connected with other executive duties were found in the same area: a purser's gauging rule with which spirits in cask were measured (56), balance-pan weights and items from the surgeon's chest (57). In addition, domestic items from this part of the ship were of a markedly higher quality in comparison with those found elsewhere, denoting their owners' higher status: fine crockery from the Continent, spirit bottles, high-quality brass and pewterware and an exquisitely turned ivory snuff-box. An unusual find was a brass Highland ring-brooch, with interlaced Celtic decoration (58). This might have been a souvenir of the campaign, or perhaps it belonged to one of the Earl of Argyll's soldiers.

That the inshore end of the site represented the ship's stern was clinched by the discovery of several lozenge-shaped pieces of mica with traces of leading round their edges. These must have come from the glazing of the stern cabin windows, as clearly seen in the Van de Velde sketch. 'Muscovy glass' (i.e. mica) is mentioned in the ship's 1678 refit, and was widely used in the navy for cabin windows and galleries until 1704, when it was replaced by glass.

Objects found towards the seaward extremity of the wreck tended to fit categories associated with the bow end of the ship. They included items of a kind to be associated with the bosun's store: rigging fittings of various types, including rope, deadeyes, blocks of various sizes and

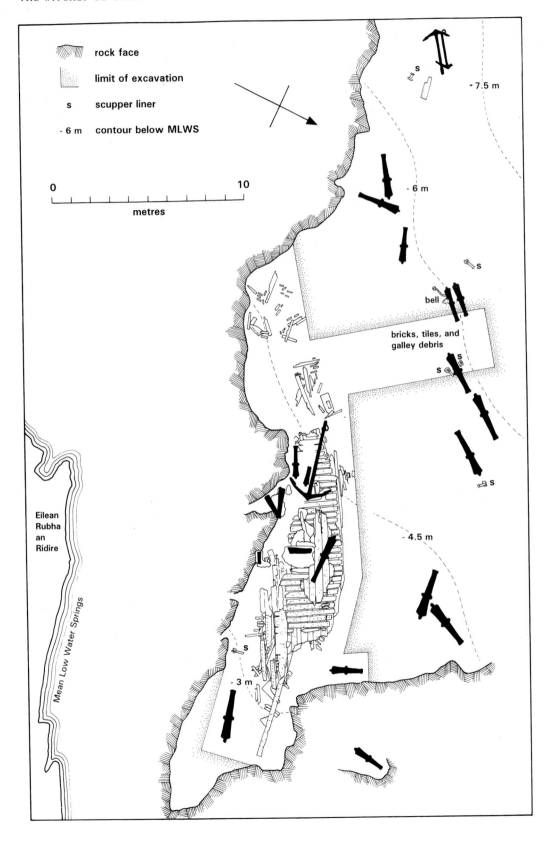

rock face

limit of excavation

s   scupper liner

- 6 m   contour below MLWS

0   10

metres

- 7.5 m

s

- 6 m

s

bell

bricks, tiles, and
galley debris

s

s

s

s

- 4.5 m

Eilean
Rubha
an
Ridire

Mean Low Water Springs

s

- 3 m

54 General plan of the *Dartmouth* wreck site.

several loose sheaves. Some of these fittings showed evidence of makeshift repair, while others by their lack of running wear had clearly never been used. This part of the site also yielded concretions of what had once been boxes or barrels of hand-grenades (**59**), together with large quantities of lead shot of pistol and musket calibre. These finds indicate the presence of an armoury or munitions store, a conclusion supported by the discovery in the same area of a Highland musket stock.

Like the bosun's locker the ship's armoury was generally situated well forward. This part of

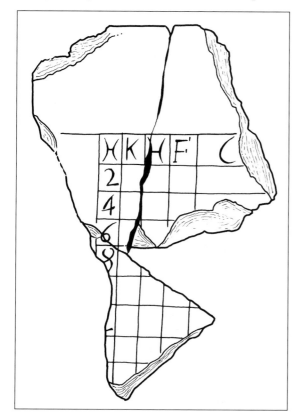

55 Fragments of a log slate (Length 9 cm (3½ in)). The left-hand column shows the two-hour watch periods marked by the bell, while 'K', 'H', and 'F' stand for knots, half-knots, and fathoms – timed distances run by the ship's log-line, from which its speed through the water was calculated. The 'C' column recorded the compass course steered.

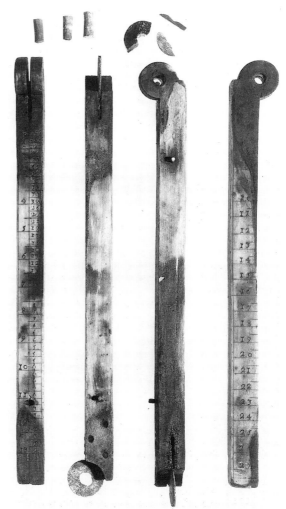

56 A boxwood folding gauger's rule, used for measuring the volume of liquids in cask.

the vessel, and the midships area, provided accommodation for the crew, and the domestic objects found here were of markedly lower quality than those associated with the stern. The relatively small quantity of pottery was made up of coarsewares, and there was no pewter. The crew, it would appear, ate mostly off square or round pieces of board.

Among the bricks and tiles of the collapsed galley were found considerable quantities of burnt debris, animal bones and coal. A concentration of clay pipes was also noted here. The only other concentration of pipes on the wreck was observed in the region of the stern,

57 A pewter syringe for the treatment of venereal disease.
Length 13 cm (5 in).

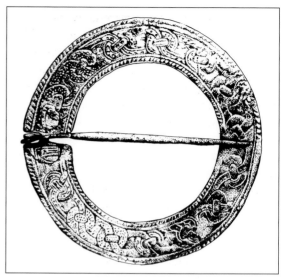

58 A Celtic ring-brooch of brass with interlaced decoration
(diameter 11.5 cm (4½ in)). This may have been a locally
acquired souvenir, or it could perhaps have belonged to
one of the Earl of Argyll's soldiers aboard the ship.

and these were of markedly higher quality. Once
again, a nice social distinction between officers
and men is apparent. Smoking was supposed to
be restricted to the galley area: not very
hygienic, perhaps, but the tile-lined cubicle in
which the cooking stove was housed provided
the only safe place on board in which to strike a
light. This sensible stricture, it would appear,
was not followed by the captain and his officers.

Many of the clay pipes bear the initials I C,
which are believed to be those of James
Colquhoun, a prolific Glasgow pipemaker
during this period. Examples of his pipes have
been found on the site of the ill-fated Scots
settlement in Darien, briefly occupied between
1698 and 1700.

Much of the surviving structure was pinned
down by several large iron concretions which
included guns, shot, and a 4 m (13 ft) anchor.

59 A hollow cast-iron grenade (scale in cm). This broken
example shows in section the wooden fuse plug and the
residue of its gunpowder charge.

That at least some of this material was ballast is suggested by the number of broken guns (old pieces were frequently used for this purpose) and by roundshot too large to fit any of the *Dartmouth*'s guns. There were also quantities of flint chippings which do not derive from the local geology, and are presumably ballast.

Ballast was an ever-present problem on ships of this kind, since it tended to accumulate dirt and rubbish, and was almost invariably wet. On 7 November 1689 William Kiggins, *Dartmouth*'s lieutenant, had written from Hoylake, Cheshire, that

> our ship's company is sickly, one great
> occasion of it is, our ballast being so bad,
> stinking and all of a quagmire, and sandy
> that it stoaks [blocks] the limbers [drainage
> holes], that the water has no course to the
> pump. Had we that ballast out, and shingle
> in, I doubt not that our ship would be
> healthy, and in good condition.

This sorry state of affairs would surely have been put to rights when Pottinger unloaded his ballast at Greenock on 26 July 1690, if not before.

Piecing together the ship

A section through the surviving remains of the hull provides a starting point for reconstructing the break-up of the ship (**60**). The remains include: oak frames, their top surfaces heavily abraded; ceiling (i.e. inner) and outer planking of elm; fir sheathing planks, and an elm keel, abraded from the bottom upwards. The lateral axis of the keel shows that the ship lay heeled over to starboard at an angle of 23 degrees.

We can reconstruct the keel's original depth from the shipwright's account of the replacement keel which was fitted to the ship in 1678. It was 13 in (0.33 m) square, and beneath it an 8 in (0.20 m) 'false' keel, or extension, had been added. The original total depth of 19 in (0.43 m) closely matches a shingle-filled trench cut into the hard substrate below the keel. This suggests that, during the wrecking process, the ship rocked from side to side on the fulcrum provided by its keel, causing it to dig deeply into the abrasive substrate. As it did so the bottom part of the keel was ground away.

Abrasion is not, however, in evidence on the surfaces of the outer planking, to which some of

60 Section through the surviving portion of the hull.

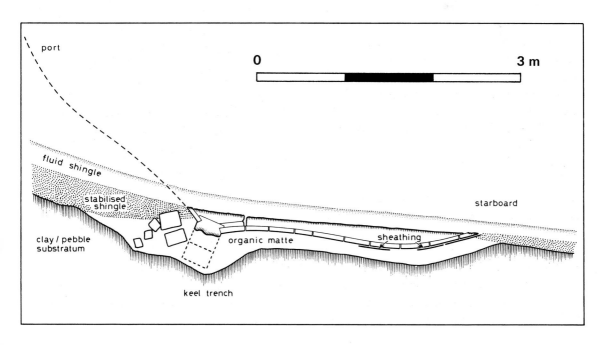

the fragile sheathing of fir boards and tarred horsehair is still attached (**61**). This outer layer was intended to deter attack by the common shipworm (*Teredo navalis*). The practice does not seem to have been all that effective, for the *Dartmouth*'s timbers are riddled with the borings and calcareous exoskeletons of this voracious mollusc.

From this evidence it appears that the wreckage dug itself into the seabed while both sides of the ship were still substantially intact, allowing water movement to rock the hull and

so cause the keel, in abrasive contact with the sea floor, to dig through the shingle and into the substratum. The starboard planking, cushioned by water and in no direct contact with the seabed, would have fanned away the shingle beneath it to form the hollow into which it eventually settled with minimal damage to its outer surfaces.

In the process a thick mat of wood splinters together with other material from the fabric and contents of the ship became incorporated beneath and around the hull remains. The keel-trench, in particular, acted as a gravity trap for metal and ceramic objects. This suggests that the ship broke up in a continuous and fairly rapid sequence, allowing structural components and other material which fell from the disintegrating upper parts of the vessel to gather at the bottom of the keel-trench before it became stabilized (**62**).

61 A naturally eroded section of the ship's structure shows (top right) closely-spaced oak frames, ground to conformity with the seabed; 3-inch main planking of elm, partially eroded towards the camera, and thin fir outer sheathing securing a layer of horsehair and pitch to deter shipworm.

Once the wreck remains had stabilized, the natural sands and gravels reasserted themselves to a depth varying from 0.6 m (20 in) to 0.15 m (5 in) or less. The moving upper levels of this material have caused considerable abrasion to the upper parts of the structure, grinding them to a flat conformity with the seabed profile. This process, slow but inexorable, would eventually have destroyed the remainder of the ship.

These articulated remains lie at the head of a V-shaped gully, the apex of which lies close inshore. This represents the stern part of the ship, as determined by artefact distribution (see above). The 6 m (20 ft) run of surviving keel stops where a spur of rock intrudes upon its axis, at approximately the midships point. Here the ship probably broke her back, aided no doubt by the pile-driving effect of the mainmast. It seems that her forward half then rolled down the slope on to its side, depositing the contents of the vessel's main deck as a linear scatter of guns, scupper-liners (63) and associated artefacts. The latter included the remains of the galley, which was located in the upper part of the forecastle, and the ship's bell.

An examination of the ship's remains has revealed much about contemporary shipbuilding

62 The keel-trench before excavation, showing timbers from the collapsed port side (left) and the surviving articulated structure (right).

63 A lead scupper-liner, which allowed water to drain from the ship's decks. It was once fitted with a non-return valve of leather. Scale 12 in (30 cm).

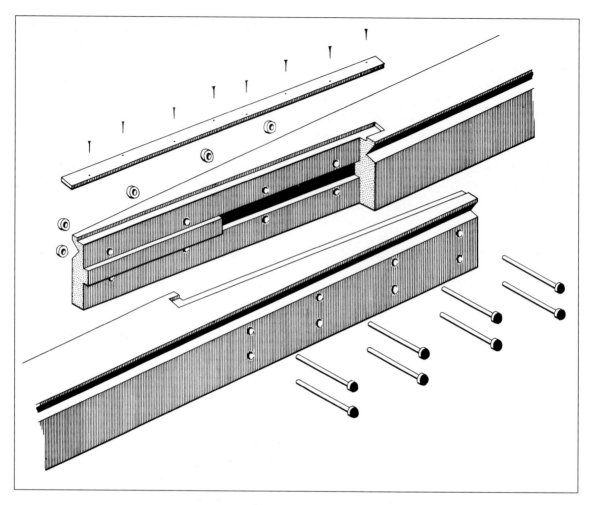

64 A reconstruction of the elaborate overlapping scarf by which sections of the elm keel were joined.

techniques. Perhaps surprisingly, little information of this kind is preserved in written sources. Most shipwrights were illiterate, and worked by tradition and rule-of-thumb. Their achievements are recorded not on paper but in the timbers of the ships they built. The solid competence and elegance of their carpentry is revealed by features such as the scarf joint which linked two sections of the keel (**64**). Documentary sources, moreover, tell us that this joint lay one-third of the overall keel length from the stern, thus providing a fixed point from which to reconstruct the *Dartmouth*'s fine after-lines.

Isolated components can tell us much about the overall construction of the ship. A lodging knee – one of the horizontal timber brackets from the main deck structure – was found loose in the keel-trench (**65** and **66**). It is a 'grown' timber, that is, it has been selected from a part of the parent oak where a major branch joins the trunk, so that the run of grain matches the shape of the piece. The knee shows that the deck structure had been built in 5-foot (1.5 m) modules, a standardized dimension reflected in contemporary ship-plans.

Even more interesting is the evidence of modification and repair which had kept this ageing ship in service far beyond her normal working life. The 1678 refit at Rotherhithe involved particularly drastic changes. Not only was the keel replaced, but the bottom parts of the frames, which were evidently rotten too, were chopped out and replaced by a massive

elm clamp bolted through to the new keel. This unconventional solution demonstrates considerable ingenuity on the part of the shipwrights, and indicates the pressure they were under to squeeze a few more years' life out of the ship.

The outer planking, too, showed evidence of frequent maintenance and repair (**67**). The 3-inch (7.6 cm) thick elm planks had originally been fastened to the frames with two trenails (wooden pegs) at each joint, arranged in a zig-zag pattern to avoid setting up lines of weakness along the grain. Over time many additional trenails had been added to tighten up the hull, especially along the three lower planks which had been replaced during the

65 A lodging knee from the upper deck structure. Scale 12 in (30 cm).

66 The author recovering the lodging knee – the weight-lessness of the underwater world has some advantages!

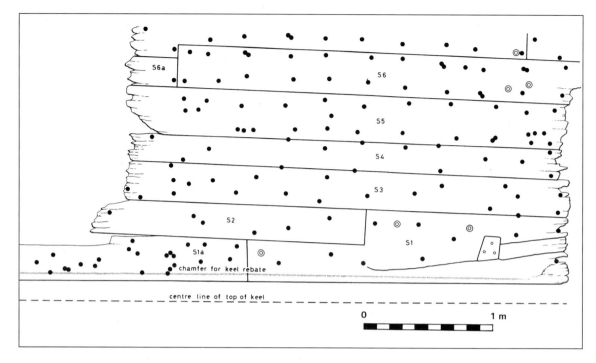

67 Diagram showing the outer planking of the lower hull, with its evidence of extensive maintenance and repair.

Rotherhithe refit. In one instance a split in the planking had been checked by cutting a trapezoidal hole in its path and plugging it with a wooden patch.

Even rigging fittings were used well beyond the time they should have been replaced. A wooden sheave from a pulley-block which had worn its bearing hole into an ellipse had been repaired, with considerable ingenuity and skill, by inserting a hardwood filling-piece to bring it back to the round. The *Dartmouth*'s crewmen were evidently doing all they could to keep their ramshackle old ship in working order right up to the end.

Only two coins were found during the excavations, but they could scarcely have been more appropriate (**colour plates 9** and **10**). Both are gold guineas. One depicts James VII and II and its date, 1687, is the last year in which this monarch minted coins. The revolution of 1688 followed and in 1689 its victors, William and Mary, issued their first coinage. The second *Dartmouth* guinea is of this date. These two coins graphically symbolize the great historical events in which the *Dartmouth* played a humble but by no means insignificant part.

A legend confirmed

A tradition of the *Dartmouth* wreck survives on Mull to the present day. It was told to the writer in 1974 by the late Willie Fletcher of Loch Don, who had himself heard it 60 years earlier from a woman then aged 80. She in turn had heard it as a child from her grandmother. The story attributes the loss of the ship to Jacobite-inspired witchcraft. At Maclean of Duart's instigation a coven of witches led by *Gormal far na Maighe* (Great Gormal from Moy) gathered in the chapel at Pennygown, not far from where the *Dartmouth* was anchored, and cast a powerful spell on the ship.

The spell required a rope to be tied through a heavy millstone and used to pull the stone over a rafter, so causing the warship anchored in the bay to heel over and sink. The analogy of the toppling millstone and the capsizing ship is particularly vivid in the story, and stress is laid on the effort needed by the witches to pull the heavy and awkwardly balanced stone over the beam. Several times it almost came over but fell back, and several times the ship heeled critically in the gale before righting herself. Finally, with the aid of the local blacksmith, the millstone was pulled over the rafter, and this time the *Dartmouth* fell on her beam ends and did not recover.

Another version of the story, recorded a century ago, states that:

> for two days it blew very hard, and the ship's anchors held during that time; but on the third day the wind was so violent that some of the cables gave way, and she drifted, pulling the anchors after her. And away she went, stern foremost, until she struck the Knight's Point in Morvern, across the Sound. The waves beat on her until she went to pieces there, to the great rejoicing of the Macleans.

Until the middle of the nineteenth century the site of the wreck was remembered locally. The Reverend Norman Macleod, writing in 1867, stated that the ship 'was wrecked on a rock opposite Duart, and only a few years ago the spot was examined ... when human remains were discovered. Some of the guns of the vessel have also, I believe, been seen.'

Though perhaps we can discount the efficacy of witchcraft in sealing the *Dartmouth*'s fate, much of the traditional story appears to be rooted in a genuine folk-memory of the event. As we have seen, the archaeological investigation has shown that the ship indeed hit Eilean Rubha an Ridire stern first. It also revealed that three anchors were on board the vessel when she was wrecked – two apparently stowed and lashed near the bow and one, the largest, still in the hold.

For a ship to leave anchors on board when she was in dire peril of wrecking on a lee shore seems extraordinary. Even allowing for a surface drift of ten knots, there would have been an interval of at least ten minutes from breaking adrift in Scallastle Bay to striking the island, time enough for desperate and skilful seamen to loose the two forward anchors. They might even have brought up, stocked and cast the big anchor stowed below – probably her sheet anchor, the *anchora spei* (anchor of hope), which was normally kept unstocked in the hold and reserved for the last extremity.

It may be that the final wrecking on Rubha an Ridire was the culmination of a series of disasters which prevented such obvious measures from being taken. The start of this fatal chain of events was probably the oversetting of the ship when the cables parted in Scallastle Bay, so vividly described by the toppling millstone analogy of the traditional story. In short, the archaeological evidence supports the vernacular accounts, in that both imply that after striking the island stern first and on her beam ends, the waves beat upon the ship 'until she went to pieces there, to the great rejoicing of the Macleans'.

5

'On Stoura Stack she broke her back' – the *Kennemerland*, 1664

'And the Skerries got a prey'

The four men clung grimly to the foremast shrouds of the scudding Dutch East Indiaman as she ran before a southerly gale through the dark December night. Six days earlier the *Kennemerland* had left the Texel in Holland for the Far East on a north-about cast around the British Isles, a route chosen to avoid contrary winds in the Channel and the vigilant warships of the Royal Navy, for Holland and Britain were at war. Now she was close to the treacherous islands and reefs of Shetland and the bedraggled quartet of lookouts, including the ship's pilot, had been posted in the shrouds to keep a watch for land.

It came upon them before they could shout a warning. With a juddering crash the 150-foot (46 m) vessel careered into a low stack of rock almost smothered by breakers. The foremast fell against the stack, allowing three of the lookouts to scramble ashore. They were the only survivors. The ship, with more than 200 people on board, then broke in half. As the forepart foundered in deep water beside the stack, spilling its ballast, the lightened stern portion was borne by the wind to fetch up high and dry a kilometre away on the beach of Bruray Island in the Out Skerries.

The dramatic details of the wrecking, as described above, are preserved in Skerries folklore, where the following rhyme is still current:

The Carmelan [*sic*] *frae Amsterdam*
Cam on a Maunsmas Day
On Stoura Stack she broke her back
And into the voe she ca'

It is reputed that the Skerry folk were drunk for three weeks on the kegs of wine and brandy that came ashore.

The wreck took place on 20 December 1664, and serious attempts at salvage were soon underway. The Earl of Morton (who was the laird of Shetland) sent his chamberlain, Robert Hunter, to take charge of affairs, and by dragging the seabed with grapnels and pole-hooks much of value was recovered. One witness recorded how, on 16 January 1665, he saw 'three chests numbered 1, 2, and 4' one of which contained '16 bags of gold, another 8, and the 3rd £2000 Scots of layed money'.

In total this amounted to nearly 115,000 of the 120,000 guilders consigned aboard the *Kennemerland*, though, unfortunately for the salvors, officialdom thought the ship had carried twice as much. The confusion arose because the full consignment being shipped to the Indies was indeed 240,000 guilders, but half of it had been loaded aboard another ship, the *Rijnland*, which had not been wrecked. Because England and Holland were in a state of war Charles II's government claimed that 'all schips belonging to the Kinges enemies ... cast away upon any of the sea coasts of this kingdome ... doth belong to his Majestie.' When the matter came to court, it

was presumed that the Earl of Morton had deliberately set out to defraud the King and, most unjustly, he was deprived of his estates.

Charles II later granted rights to salvage the wreck to the Earl of Kincardine, and it appears that some further recoveries were made.

The *Kennemerland* wreck today

The remains of the *Kennemerland* were located in 1971 by a team of divers from the Aston University Sub-Aqua Club. Between that time and 1987 six further seasons of archaeological work were conducted on the site, co-ordinated by Richard Price (**68**). In the 1970s the wreck was used as a proving ground by the late Keith Muckelroy in his pioneering work on wreck

68 A surface-supplied diver operating a metal detector among the thick kelp jungle which blankets the *Kennemerland* wreck site.

formation studies. His interest focused on the complex interrelationships between underwater archaeological depositions and their environments, which he rightly saw as keys to understanding the processes of wrecking. This work has been continued more recently by Christopher Dobbs of the *Mary Rose* Trust.

Muckelroy's research was based on concepts which he labelled as 'extractive filters', which remove or destroy archaeological material, and 'scrambling devices', which rearrange what is left. Extractive filters can be divided into three categories. The first operates during the physical event of the shipwreck, when much material is lost through the influences of wind, waves and currents. What reaches the seabed is then exposed to a second extractive filter: chemical and biological degradation. Human interference – whether by salvors or archaeologists – constitutes a third filter which may remove material from the site.

These filtering processes, though often complex and difficult to interpret, are relatively straightforward to comprehend. It is harder to quantify the nature and effects of the scrambling devices. The first is the process of wrecking itself. In the case of the *Kennemerland* the broad outline can be deduced from the deposition of wreck material on the seabed, supplemented by the traditional account (69). The impact area around the base of Stoura Stack is characterized by a spill of thousands of bricks and more than 100 lead ingots, which dropped from the lower hold when the ship broke apart. Six anchors have also been found in this area.

Much of the upper structure of the vessel and its contents was then carried across the bay by the southerly gale, grounding where the rocky seabed rises to within 10 m (32 ft) of the surface, about 150 m (160 yds) from the first impact. Here a secondary break-up took place, depositing more bricks and a concentration of other cargo. Even so, enough structural integrity was still maintained by part of the hull to carry six iron cannons further towards the shore, dropping them in a linear scatter as far as the islet of Trolsome, 200 m (215 yds) away. According to the traditional story, much wreckage was finally thrown up on the main island, Bruray, although no archaeological manifestation of this final movement has yet been noted.

A second scrambling factor is the post-depositional movement of wreck material across the seabed or within its sediments. Tidal regimes within the bay and across its mouth are complex and, at times, powerful. It is possible that at least one part of the broken ship, having first entered the bay, was subsequently swept out of it, as suggested by the find of two isolated cannons in deep water to the south of the primary impact point. Within the main depositions, moreover, current movement over the seabed has had the effect of burying objects, and of re-sorting them over time. Even marine flora and fauna have may have helped to move artefacts across the sea floor, as evidenced by the kelp-propelled pottery observed at the *Swan* site. It has even been suggested that clay pipe-bowls might move considerable distances as the portable dwellings of hermit crabs!

A cargo for the Indies

Between 1971 and 1987 several seasons of excavation were conducted on the *Kennemerland* site. Most of the work concentrated on the deposition just inside the mouth of the voe, where much of the ship's cargo appears to have dropped. Excavation was carried out on a systematic basis using a grid system, mostly by hand, although at times a light water-dredge was employed.

The finds provided a rich sampling of the ship's varied cargo. Among the most remarkable was a salt-glazed Rhenish flagon, with its characteristic 'Bellarmine' facemask and heraldic escutcheon, which proved to contain 18 kg (40 lb) of mercury. This dense liquid metal was difficult to transport, and it is likely that the flagon had been wrapped in straw or some similar packing material and contained within a box. Mercury was used for the refining of silver, and for medical purposes. Several more Bellarmine flagons were found, one of which contained a number of peach stones (**colour plate 11**).

Pottery was widely scattered over the wreck site, as were the remains of bottles. Most were of the square 'case' variety (normally carried in compartmented wooden cases which held a dozen) associated with Dutch gin. They were fitted with pewter screw-tops, many of which were found on the wreck.

Clay pipes were another common item aboard East Indiamen, and a find from Western

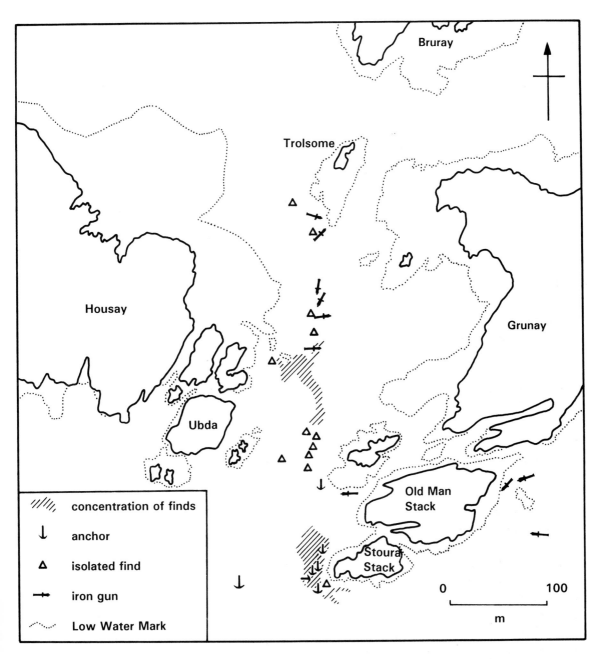

69 General plan of the *Kennemerland* wreck site.

Australia shows that they were packed head-to-tail in wooden boxes filled with buckwheat. The examples from the *Kennemerland*, however, demonstrate a considerable variety of forms and markings, which suggests that the pipes may have been owned by individuals for their own use, or as items for private trade. One stem

comes from a well-known type showing a monster devouring a man, variously interpreted as depicting Jonah and the whale or Walter Raleigh being swallowed by a crocodile. All were probably made in Gouda.

Private trade was almost certainly the purpose of a remarkable group of finds made in this area. It includes ornately-engraved tobacco-boxes (**70**), cheap brass rings, pewter pendants and brass

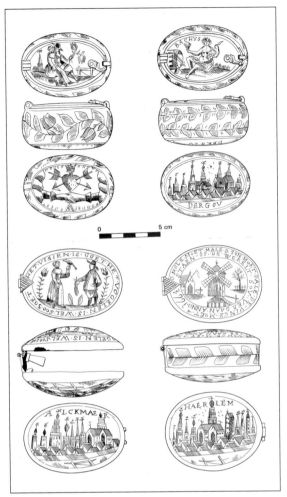

70 Brass tobacco-boxes.

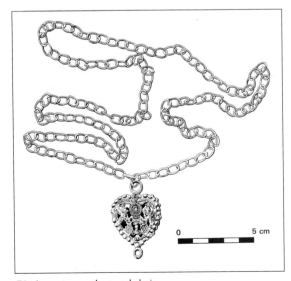

71 A pewter pendant and chain.

janglers on chains (71), brass bodkins, lace bobbins, thimbles (72), dice (73), two pocket sundials (74) and five pewter golf-club heads (75). Such mass-produced items from the cheap end of the luxury market are not the kind of things that appear in East Indiamen's cargo manifests, and their discovery as a discrete group suggests that they are more probably from an individual

72 A brass thimble. Scale in mm.

73 Bone dice. Each is approximately 1 cm square.

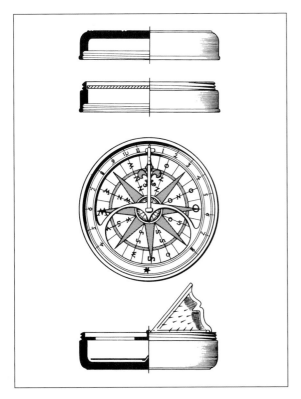

74 A pocket compass/sundial of brass. Diameter 4.5 cm (1¾ in). The printed compass card has survived in almost perfect condition.

seaman's trading chest. A box-load of such light and relatively inexpensive European baubles would have yielded high profits to an enterprising private trader in the markets of the East.

The tobacco-boxes are remarkable social documents, for both their lids and bases are engraved with lively scenes. Three show townscapes of Haarlem, Alkmar and Gouda. One box has a charming representation of a peasant couple courting and a love symbol of clasped hands and a heart pierced by arrows. Another scene shows a suitably dissipated Bacchus with wine glass, grapes and cask.

There are two representations of Dutch sayings. One shows a windmill, a tree and a house from the upper window of which an unidentified article (a flag or fish?) dangles from a pole. Around the edge is an inscription which translates: 'The mill must grind, the sun must sink, or the world must end. 1664'. The date, it will be noted, is that of the wreck. The other depicts a man holding a fish and a woman holding a bird, with the enigmatic and slightly suggestive inscription: 'The fishing is good, the fowling is sweet as well'.

One of the pocket sundials is in virtually perfect condition, including the compass card with its coloured markings. It consists of three brass sections which screw together to form, at the base, a container for the compass; a piece which holds the glass face, an hour-ring, a folding gnomon and a lid. Such instruments originated in southern Germany around 1400. The user oriented himself with the compass, erected the gnomon and read the time from the shadow.

It was a laborious and not very reliable process which only worked in the hemisphere and latitude for which the instrument had been calibrated, and then only if local magnetic variation was accurately known. The *Kennemerland* sundial's gnomon has a centre angle of 52 degrees, appropriate to the latitude of the Low Countries. In the Far East it would have been useless except perhaps as a symbol of Western technology, akin to the proverbial Cadillac in a country without roads.

The five golf-club heads from the *Kennemerland* are among the earliest known – a few have been associated with a late sixteenth-

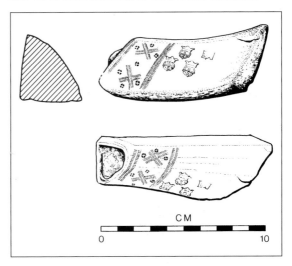

75 A pewter golf-club head.

76 Part of the *Kennemerland's* cargo of lead ingots being weighed for analysis.

77 Various marks stamped on the ingots include the initials M R and the date 1664 – the year the ship was lost. Scale in cm.

century context in Amsterdam, while four others were recovered from the wreck of the Dutch East Indiaman *Lastdrager* (1653), also wrecked in Shetland (see p. 113). Three of the *Kennemerland* clubs were for left-handed players. Golf seems to have originated during the later medieval period on the western seaboards of Holland and Zealand, and at an early date was exported to Scotland by sailors and merchants. The finds from the *Lastdrager* and *Kennemerland* suggest that it was a popular game among Dutch expatriates in the Far East too.

78 Bow-headed navigator's dividers. The design, which is still used today, permitted the instrument to be operated with one hand. Length 11.5 cm (4_ in).

Personal objects might either have been the property of those on board, or cargo bound for the Indies. They include bone combs, pewter spoons, knives, a scabbard and shoes. The 60 or so silver coins, mainly ducatons, will likewise either have belonged to individuals on board or be part of the ship's consignment of treasure – though, as we have seen, most of the latter appears to have been recovered by contemporary salvors. A cased padlock of brass once, no doubt, secured a box containing valuables.

As with the *Adelaar* (see p. 104), the *Kennemerland*'s ballast was carried in the form of building bricks and lead ingots (**76** and **77**).

Ship's equipment

Very little of the ship's fabric has survived in the exposed seabed around Stoura Stack, although some fragments of timber and rope have been preserved in small protected pockets, or in concretion. Several objects, however, relate to activities aboard the ship. The most important of these is navigation, represented by dividers (**78**), sounding leads and part of the earliest known example of a backstaff, an instrument used for calculating latitude. There is also a brass hour-ring which was once fitted to a small terrestrial globe, to indicate the time of day in different parts of the world at any given moment.

Two pewter syringes, similar to those recovered from the *Dartmouth* (see p. 76), no doubt came from the surgeon's chest. Medicine at sea was an important aspect of shipboard life, and quite complex surgical procedures were sometimes performed. The *Lastdrager* wreck, for example, has produced part of a brass wimble used for skull trepanation.

Routine maintenance of tools and weapons no doubt consumed much of the time of those on board, and such activities are represented by a grindstone and a mould for casting lead shot. Officially-attested weights remind us of the carefully-controlled issue of daily rations.

Of those rations little has survived except the peach stones noted above, some plum stones, a few cattle and sheep bones, and a small cache of peppercorns. The latter, we may suppose, were on their second voyage half-way round the world, for they must originally have come to Europe in the hold of a homeward-bound East Indiaman.

6

The wreck on Cursed Rock – the *Adelaar*, 1728

'The ship intirely beat to pieces'
On the evening of 23 March 1728 the minister and chamberlain of North Uist stood on the western machair looking out over the Atlantic. The object of their attention was a majestic three-masted sailing ship which flew the Dutch tricolour overlaid with the VOC monogram of the *Verenigde Oostindische Compagnie* (Dutch East India Company) (**79**). She appeared to be in no distress but she was dangerously close to the shore, and the watchers realized that if the gentle north-north-westerly breeze moved further into the west the ship would be in serious danger. The next morning she was nowhere to be seen, but the strengthening wind had shifted to west-south-west – a direction which made the entire 120 mile (195 km)-long Outer Hebridean chain a death trap for any vessel caught too close to its western side. At dusk a sudden gale came howling out of the Atlantic, and continued unabated all night.

At dawn on Monday 25 March the inhabitants of Greian, a tiny hamlet close to Barra's north-westerly headland, ventured out to see whether any flotsam had been brought ashore by the storm. To their amazement they found the rocks and beaches on either side of the headland covered with shattered baulks of timber, tangled rigging, broken casks and scores of corpses. The source of the wreckage was a hideously exposed reef on the north side of Greian Head, and during the night a large vessel had evidently struck it (**80**). For those on board

there had been no hope of survival. Among the bodies thrown grotesquely on the rocks was 'a Woman with two Children, the one tied before and the other behind; also a young Gentlewoman, who had in her Breast between her Shift and her Skin, a Letter of Recommendation from her Mother to a Gentlewoman in the East Indies'.

In 1728 the island was owned by Roderick Macneil, who was (or so he claimed) 39th in an unbroken lineage of hereditary clan chieftains. The power of the Macneil, at least within the confines of his island fastness, was absolute. It was said that each evening when the chief had finished supper his piper would call out from the battlements of Kisimul Castle to the world's lesser potentates, informing them that they might now sit down and dine (**81**).

A report later sent to George II described Barra as 'famous even in the Highlands for being barbarous' because its remoteness placed it beyond the effective rule of law. Civil jurisdiction was the technical prerogative of the sheriff at Inverness, but the great distance '& that too by sea' prevented the exercise of his authority there. The same applied to criminal law, for which the Duke of Argyll or his Deputy was responsible. Courts were simply not practicable 'without carrying over such force as would be sufficient to maintain the authority of Judicial Proceedings' and so, to all intents and purposes, Roderick Macneil was indeed above the law.

79 A contemporary model of the Dutch East Indiaman *Padmos*, built for the Zeeland Chamber of the company in 1721. Her specifications closely match those of the *Adelaar*.

At the time of the incident he was in Harris, courting his future bride, Alice Macleod of Luskentyre, but when a messenger arrived from Barra with news of the wreck, romance took second place. Within 24 hours the Macneil was back on his island, having carefully bypassed the house of Alexander Macdonald of Boisdale at Kilbride on South Uist, close to the Barra ferry. Boisdale, younger son of the chief of the Clanranald Macdonalds, had links with the authorities on the mainland, and was clearly to be avoided; in any case the Barra Macneils and Uist Clanranalds held each other in hereditary mistrust. Once safely on Barra, the Macneil placed guards at the ferry and ordered that no one was to enter or leave the island. He then set about organizing the pillage of the wreck.

For a week the Barra people gathered up what had been cast ashore and stripped the dead of valuables and clothing. By the following Sunday, however, timbers from the wrecked ship had begun to wash up on South Uist. Boisdale, his suspicions already aroused by the

80 Mollachdag – the Cursed Rock – where the *Adelaar* was wrecked. Most of her remains lie between the large rock and the shore.

81 Kisimul Castle, stronghold of the Macneil of Barra.

unprecedented lack of ferry traffic from Barra, sent a boat to investigate. On its return with news of the wreck he crossed to Greian with three boatloads of his kinsmen, all armed to the teeth. Alexander Macdonald of Boisdale was determined to exercise his rights and responsibilities as Admiral Substitute for the Western Isles.

These rights he held on behalf of Alexander Mackenzie, Younger of Delvine (an estate in Perthshire). Mackenzie was a member of the Edinburgh legal establishment and, among his many sinecures, he was Admiral Depute for the Western Isles. This authority gave him the right to salvage wrecks within his area of responsibility, and in turn depended upon the patronage of Scotland's High Admiral, the Duke of Queensberry. The laws of admiralty (the term in this connection being related to civil maritime law rather than to naval matters) were complex and virtually uncodified, depending on custom and precedent for their execution. Boisdale thus found himself responsible for administering law of which he had only the haziest knowledge on an island whose proprietor recognized no authority but his own.

There was a tense confrontation at the wreck site. The stripped corpses were still unburied after more than a week, and the Macneil informed Boisdale that 'if he was to take the goods as Admiral, he behoved to carry the Bodies to Uist also.' But after 'a great deal of struigle' it was agreed that the Macneil should retain a third of what had been recovered and deliver the balance to the Substitute Admiral. In fact, the point was academic, for everything had been spirited away and no islander would admit to the slightest knowledge of where it might now be.

All this was duly reported by Boisdale to his superior in Edinburgh, Admiral Depute Alexander Mackenzie. In response Mackenzie sent his brother-in-law Eugene Fotheringham, a Leith merchant and shipmaster, to Barra. When Fotheringham reached the island he found that the Macneil had gone 'off to some Small Isles belonging to him on the south of Barra where he skulked as long as the Gentleman stayed on the Island'. Of Barra's remaining population (estimated at around 1300 in the 1760s) only three elderly people could be found. From them, however, Fotheringham obtained some documents which had come ashore in a chest. He also made a careful survey of the wreck site. Although he noted its exposed location – 'all surrounded with steep rocks inaccessible to the smallest boat, and the places where most [wreckage] was lying were so surrounded with rocks over which the sea broke even in the best weather' – he also observed that the wreck was quite shallow, most of it lying in 4 to 6 fathoms of clear water.

The papers obtained by Fotheringham identified the ship and her contents. She was the Dutch East Indiaman *Adelaar* (Eagle), bound from Middelburg to Batavia (modern Jakarta, in Indonesia) with a general cargo of cloth, domestic hardware, and tools, and a large consignment of treasure with which to purchase the return cargo of spices, tea and porcelain. As paying ballast she carried lead ingots and 60,000 yellow bricks, which were to be used for building houses of the distinctive Dutch type which are still to be seen at the Cape and at Jakarta. One tantalizing document itemized the treasure in detail. It was a receipt, dated 6 March 1728, signed by Captain Willem de Keyser and Chief Merchant Simon Pieter Troillaert for 500 8-mark bars of silver, each stamped with the company monogram, six bars of gold, 32,000 silver ducatons struck that year at Middelburg, and 450,000 2-stuyver copper coins. The specie was packed into 17 numbered chests, after which 'two locks were hung on each chest whereof the key of each lock from chest to chest was taken by us and sealed with our usual seal and bound with cords.' The keys were placed in the last chest, which contained the gold bars.

The *Adelaar* had been built in the Middelburg yards of the company's Zeeland chamber in 1722. Her dimensions (in

Amsterdam feet of about 11 imperial inches) were standard for a medium-sized vessel on the Indies route: length 145 ft (40.2 m), beam 37 ft (10.5 m) and laden draught 15½ ft (4.4 m). Her displacement was about 700 tonnes. To protect her from European enemies she carried 36 muzzle-loading guns – ten 12-pounders, twenty 6-pounders and six 3-pounders. These were of Swedish cast iron except the two 6-pounders adjacent to the compasses, which were of bronze to reduce magnetic deviation. Eight light breech-loading swivel guns of a type generally regarded as obsolete in Europe at the time were mounted on her upper works to counter the threat of small-boat piracy in Asian waters.

Between 1722 and 1727 the *Adelaar* made two round-trips to Batavia, the VOC's fortified post on the north coast of Java. Both voyages were uneventful, with exceptionally low death rates on the outward legs of two and four respectively. In December 1727 the ship was commissioned for a third voyage under Willem de Keyser of Middelburg. It was to be his second command on this prestigious and lucrative run – in 1725/6 he had taken the *Everswaart* to Batavia and back. Early in 1728 Simon Pieter Troillaert was appointed supercargo, the on-board merchant for the voyage. He would remain at Batavia in the company's service, and was to be accompanied by his wife and child.

Other executive members of the crew included the three mates, a surgeon, and a *ziekentrooster*, or lay chaplain. About 20 passengers – mainly company officials and their families – also sailed with the ship. Sixty company soldiers under Captain Pieter Jansen were allocated to the *Adelaar* for protection during the voyage and subsequent service in the Indies. Their names and places of origin survive as a muster-roll, which also indicates that each was allowed to take with him a chest of personal trade goods. Only 21 were Dutch, the rest coming from Germany or the southern Netherlands.

Information about the 120 seamen is less complete, being restricted to those who wanted to allocate their wages to dependants ashore or to people (usually women) from whom they had borrowed money to sponsor their trade chests. Dutchmen predominate, though sailors from Bergen, Stockholm, Jutland, Hamburg, Riga, Danzig, Bremen, Lubeck, Brandenburg, Revel, Copenhagen, Venice and the Levant are recorded. The ship's carpenter was Daniel More of Lerwick.

On 21 March the *Adelaar* sailed from the roadstead at Rammekens and headed into the North Sea, intent on a north-about passage around the British Isles. Two weeks later she struck Greian Head.

Coming of the wrackmen

When Eugene Fotheringham returned to Edinburgh in mid July with the stunning news that the wreck off Barra was a treasure-laden East Indiaman, Alexander Mackenzie began drawing together a remarkable plan to salvage it. First he sought the opinions of Scotland's most senior lawyers, Charles Erskine and Duncan Forbes of Culloden, Solicitor-General and Lord Advocate respectively, regarding his rights as Admiral Depute. Could he take an armed force to Barra to ensure that the processes of admiralty law could be applied in the face of the Macneil's stated refusal to recognize it? This worried the cautious Erskine, though Forbes's opinion was robustly affirmative. And what about the rights of the Dutch, as owners of the wrecked goods? Erskine and Forbes both considered that while the Dutch would retain their right to a proportion of the property should it be recovered, they could not interfere with the Admiral Depute's efforts to salvage it.

Finally, what if the Dutch came with authority to salvage the wreck from the King and Council in London? The two Scots lawyers were in firm agreement on this point. Neither the King nor his ministers in London had the authority to over-ride Scottish admiralty jurisdiction in this respect, so the matter could not arise.

Encouraged by this advice, Mackenzie embarked upon his scheme to recover the treasure. He had little capital of his own, for as heir to Delvine his resources were in anticipated property, not cash. But his rights of admiralty were, he believed, as good as money in the bank, and he had access to a wide network of contacts and influence, based on family ties and past favours. The issue of shares in a joint-stock enterprise could purchase all the services he required. He found a ready backer in his brother-in-law Eugene Fotheringham, who put up the initial stake in return for a fifth share in the recoveries.

A 25-ton sloop, the *Grizel* of Leith, was purchased and fitted out for sea under the command of John Hay. Fotheringham was made joint master and given a commission of Substitute Admiralty which empowered him to act independently on Mackenzie's behalf. Since Barra 'scarce affords the necessities of life to the Inhabitants', the sloop was victualled for a long expedition (a supply of candles being the most expensive item), and to disguise its real intentions a cargo of meal was loaded into the hold. Financial backing for the voyage and cargo was obtained from Alexander Tait, an Edinburgh merchant to whom Mackenzie was related on his mother's side. At this stage Tait was not apparently made aware of the venture's true purpose.

Recovery of the treasure from the 4 to 6 fathoms in which it lay required divers, and through his association with admiralty matters Mackenzie was familiar with the work which was being undertaken that summer on the Armada wreck *El Gran Grifón* off Fair Isle by the two English 'wrackmen', Captain Jacob Rowe and William Evans, in Rowe's patented diving engine (see pp. 23–4 and 35). At the end of July Fotheringham and Hay departed for the northern isles to seek out and engage the divers 'on such terms as the Substitute should learn to be the practice in the like cases'.

The *Grizel* put into Stromness, and after some difficulty contact was made with Rowe and Evans. The hoped-for treasure at Fair Isle had failed to materialize, and they were more than willing to join Mackenzie's expedition. But Rowe claimed exclusive rights 'in all the British seas' for his diving engine, and drove a hard bargain. On 19 August a contract was signed at Stromness which reserved Fotheringham's one-fifth gross and gave a third of the remainder to Rowe and Evans, payable in kind on recovery. Costs were to be split between the parties. Rowe also insisted on using his own salvage sloop, the *Charming Jenny*, for transporting his crew and equipment to Barra.

Back in Edinburgh Mackenzie had been laying plans to neutralize any Macneil resistance to the salvage operation by invoking what he believed to be his right (reinforced by Forbes's opinion, but not by Erskine's) to call out the lieges in support of his admiralty jurisdiction on Barra. The lieges he had in mind were Boisdale's Clanranalds from South Uist and Benbecula, who were under obligation to him and his family. Ranald Macdonald, the late Captain of Clanranald, had been out in the '15 rebellion and afterwards suffered forfeiture of his estates and exile at St Germain. During the early 1720s, Mackenzie's father negotiated Ranald's pardon and the restoration of his estates. But before he could return to Scotland the chief died at St Germain without issue, and the chieftainship passed to Donald Macdonald of Benbecula. He was Alexander Macdonald of Boisdale's father.

This connection enabled Alexander Mackenzie to mobilize 150 'Gentlemen of the Country of South Uist with their travelling weapons' for the Barra expedition on a promise of £1500, to be paid when the treasure was recovered. Because the Disarming Act of 1725 prohibited Scotsmen from bearing weapons except those worn by gentlemen for personal defence on the road, it seems that Mackenzie's words were chosen with care. They implied that the raised lieges were no more than a body of gentry wearing legal sidearms for their journey to Barra in support of law and order. The reality was undoubtedly quite different: a pack of

Clanranald hard-men led by their chieftain's younger son, dirks and pistols at their belts and broadswords on their backs, bent on repaying a family debt of honour with the added inducement of Dutch silver and a chance to mix it with the Macneils.

To Alexander Mackenzie, educated at St Andrews University for a legal career in Edinburgh and life on a Perthshire estate, the West Highlands were unfamiliar and threatening territory. 'As I want the language and am ignorant of the roads,' he wrote to his brother Kenneth on 30 July, 'I would wish to have a Discreet Pretty Fellow in my Company.' Soon afterwards he left for Barra with 20 companions including his brother John, George Fotheringham (another brother-in-law), and James Stewart, the Gaelic-speaking 'Pretty Fellow' whose services he had sought. They travelled by Fort William (no doubt encountering General Wade's roadmakers on the way) and through Clanranald country to Loch nan Uamh before embarking for Canna. There they remained windbound until Rowe and Eugene Fotheringham, who by this time had reached South Uist, heard of their plight and came to pick them up. By late August everything was in place on Barra: the two sloops, Boisdale's private army, Mackenzie's admiralty rights, and Captain Rowe's diving team. The outsmarted Macneil offered no resistance, though he subsequently exacted a modest revenge by selling boats and local produce to the expedition at greatly inflated prices.

The diving engine could operate in water up to 10 fathoms deep and the *Adelaar's* wreckage, including the treasure, lay in less than 6 fathoms. But the site was terribly exposed. It is open to a 90-degree arc of uninterrupted Atlantic swell which breaks over the reef even when the rest of the ocean appears calm. Archaeological investigation has shown that the main area of wreckage lies within a steep-sided gully on the shore side of the reef, and it is in here that the bulk of the 1728 operations must have been conducted (**82**). Even with modern

82 Most of the *Adelaar's* contents, including the treasure, fell into this deeply fissured gully on the inshore side of Mollachdag.

diving equipment the site is hazardous and unpredictable, prone to violent surges and explosions of white water when the sea breaks over the reef's central rock. Rowe's cumbersome engine and its supporting boat would have been unimaginably difficult and dangerous to handle in such a situation, made all the worse by the tangle of masts and cordage which filled the gully and 'a great number of iron cannon two whereof lay on top of a rock which was dry at Low Water'.

All these difficulties were heroically overcome. During September, in spite of 'a long track of bad weather upon ane high and inaccessible coast [Alexander Mackenzie] did with great hazard to his own & the lives of these Gentlemen did venture out in the Sloop along with the Divers and did cause dive and fish up the goods.' By the beginning of October the bulk of the *Adelaar's* treasure had been brought safely ashore.

The Scottish case

Mackenzie's and Rowe's affairs now called them from Barra, though they were 'sensible that there were still more money and other valuable Effects' which might be recovered. At Eriskay on 5 October instructions were given to William Evans and John Hay to continue working on the wreck throughout the winter – a 'melancholy prospect' for which they and their men were given extra financial inducements (on account, naturally). Regular reports were to be submitted to Mackenzie via Boisdale, who was to keep them supplied with provisions and other necessities.

On 19 October several cart-loads of Dutch treasure rattled through the cobbled streets of Edinburgh to the Bank of Scotland, under Alexander Mackenzie's watchful eye. But he was not at home on the morning of 28 October when James Lindsay, the Admiral Macer, thrust a summons into the lockhole of his front door and knocked 'six several audible knocks' upon it. A similar document was delivered to the governor and directors of the Bank of Scotland in the 'presence of tellers and others'. The Duke of Queensberry, to whom a third summons was to be delivered, was furth of Scotland and so 'three several oysses' for him were cried at the Mercat Cross in Edinburgh and on the pier and shore of Leith. The Lords Directors of the VOC's Zeeland Chamber were suing the Lord Admiral of Scotland and his deputy in their own court for the restitution of the recovered treasure.

In May reports of the *Adelaar's* loss had reached the VOC's agent in London, and he had passed the information to Middelburg. The Dutch were slow to respond and it was not until

August that a Scottish shipmaster, David Stevenson, was engaged by the Directors of the Zeeland Chamber to pursue their interests in Barra. Meanwhile the Dutch envoy in London obtained letters of protection from George II. These stated what less than a month earlier Scottish legal opinion had so confidently asserted could not be stated – that it was proper

> to show the readiness of the Ministry to assist the Dutch East India Company, that a Letter be writ to the Duke of Queensberry that he may order his Deputies to give those who the Dutch shall employ all the Countenance & protection they can ... Mr. Wade likewise may be ordered, in case it may be necessary to send some Soldiers aboard the Vessels employed in this business to protect the Dutch from any insults.

By then it was too late – perhaps fortunately so. What might have been the outcome had General Wade's troops, charged with upholding foreign interests on behalf of the Crown, come face to face with Boisdale's armed Clanranalds whose clear duty was to resist them on the authority of Scotland's admiralty law?

The case was heard before Judge James Graham of Airth and took 30 days of court sittings, between 6 November 1728 and 11 July the following year. Charles Erskine, the Solicitor-General, led for the VOC. Alexander Mackenzie's defence was conducted by Hugh Forbes, Robert Dundas, and others, including his brother Kenneth. At first Mackenzie was equivocal about what he had recovered, but admitted to possessing 328 bars of silver, 59 bags of stuyvers, and 300 ducatons. From the outset the VOC asserted its absolute right to the treasure but accepted that Mackenzie's expenses and a salvage award should be paid. The Dutch argument turned on the extent of those expenses, profound dissatisfaction with Mackenzie's cavalier approach to accounting, and a well-founded suspicion that not all of the treasure had been declared.

Although the Lord Admiral and the Bank of Scotland were technically his co-defendants, Alexander Mackenzie was for all practical purposes on his own. At first he sought to demolish the Dutch claim in its entirety. What proof was there that the ship had been the *Adelaar*? Moreover, since no living creature had survived to maintain a continuity of possession, had the vessel and its contents not irrevocably been abandoned by its owners? On both grounds, he argued, his claim was unassailable.

The question of abandonment gave rise to some nice legal debate. All agreed that no one had survived the wreck, but much consideration was given to the status a hypothetical dog might have enjoyed had it come ashore alive. Would it, until relieved of the responsibility by the arrival of a VOC representative, have retained possession of the company's interests? And if this were so, might the same have applied had the survivor been a cat, or even a mouse? Reference was made to a precedent set in 1622 when an ox, as the sole survivor of a shipwreck, was held to have maintained a continuity of ownership 'because by the Ox the Owners may be known'.

Clear confirmation of the wreck's identity finally arrived from Middelburg on the backs of two playing cards, which bore impressions in sealing wax of the dies which had been used to strike ducatons that year in the Zeeland mint (**colour plate 12**). The issues of 1728 were the first coins to bear the Company's bale-mark, and the *Adelaar*'s consignment of 32,000 ducatons, like those recovered from the wreck, were exclusively of this type. No other vessel on which similar coins had been shipped was unaccounted for. 'Without any foreign assistance,' the concluding argument ran, 'the specie bears unbiased witness of the property in question and at the same time affords a proof who are owners of the ship.'

Because so many aspects of the case were unprecedented – not least the use of diving apparatus to effect the recoveries – much legal time was spent in studying ancient maritime codes. An act passed by James I in 1429 which laid down that a foreign ship wrecked in Scottish waters should be treated as a Scottish ship would have been treated had it been lost on the shores of the wrecked ship's nation was regarded as particularly significant by both sides. The VOC's counsel naturally emphasized the friendly generosity which a Zeeland court would have shown to the owners of a Scottish wreck; equally predictably, Mackenzie's lawyers sought to argue that the Dutch would seize everything for themselves. Judgment was eventually made in the VOC's favour, with expenses and salvage payable to the defendants.

The question of determining these now arose. Captain Rowe had already been paid his full due ('there was no cheapening the matter with him'), and Mackenzie claimed to have spent £13,926 on the project. This left a balance of only £733. The VOC strongly disputed these figures, arguing that 'the Defender should be more particular ... even though he had thought himself not accountable.' After heavy pressure from the court Mackenzie admitted to an additional 10,000 ducatons, 172 silver bars, and the six bars of gold. This accounted for the ingot specie in full, and left a shortfall of only 1700 of the 32,000 ducatons. The total estimate of the recovered treasure's value now stood at £23,500.

In the end the VOC had to pay the costs of the action, including a tax of 10 per cent 'sentence money', and Mackenzie was allowed his expenses. The treasure was not, however, immediately released. While the case had been proceeding, a counter-suit against the VOC was lodged by Captain Alexander Hamilton, who claimed that his ship had been confiscated by the Dutch 17 years earlier for alleged opium trafficking in the East Indies. His suit was eventually rejected by the House of Lords on 4 April 1732, after which the *Adelaar*'s much-depleted treasure at last returned to Holland.

Mackenzie lost heavily on the judgment. His catalogue of expenses, though clearly in part fictitious, concealed monstrous financial naïvety and a propensity, in the excitement and urgency of events, to make promises and payments he could neither honour nor afford. There were many creditors. Perhaps because of family ties Eugene Fotheringham laid no claim in court to his promised fifth, but Alexander Tait, who had sponsored the voyage to Barra in ignorance of its true purpose, vigorously pursued a claim of £1000. Although he eventually reduced this to £500, it was still unpaid by 1730 when he was seeking damages as well.

Mackenzie's financial embarrassment and the dashing of his expectations undoubtedly lay behind the harsh and hypocritical attitude he adopted towards his former associates, John Hay and William Evans, who had been left on Barra to continue working over the winter. In spite of considerable hardship they had recovered 5951 more ducatons as well as lead ingots, rope, brass, ironware, and some broken casks of rotten meat. Apparently in an attempt to deprive Hay and Evans of their promised share, Mackenzie, backed by Jacob Rowe, accused them of extravagant living and embezzlement. On 28 January 1730 Evans wrote to Mackenzie with undisguised contempt and anger on hearing of

> Mr Hay's malicious and undeserved imprisonment, he being a man that stood up soe much for your honour and reputation far beyond what you deserved ... in my opinion you are not capable of making him satisfaction for the service he has done you and the heardship he has suffered in your Dishonorable service.

By then Mackenzie was in no position to give satisfaction to anyone. The previous year, in a desperate attempt to recover his fortune, he had used his rights of admiralty together with those granted by the Crown to the Duke of Argyll in respect of the Tobermory wreck, to engage with Captain Rowe in a venture to recover its elusive (because illusory) treasure (see p. 23–25). It had ended in total failure and a new crop of debts: '... if I once had wrought my way out of this

perhaps I will take a little more care of myself in time comeing,' he wrote despairingly to his brother John on 23 April 1731, '& I hope you may also learn a lesson from it also with this advantage that it is not att your own but my expense that you'll grow wise.'

Alexander Mackenzie inherited Delvine in 1731, but with annuities payable to 12 surviving siblings (eight of them sisters, including five who never married) and a mother who was to outlive him, his finances were beyond recovery. The estate was transferred to John before Alexander died, bankrupt and blind, in 1737.

Macdonald of Boisdale stood briefly in the spotlight of history in 1745 as the man 'who spoke very disparagingly' to the Young Pretender when he landed on Eriskay, and refused to bring the Clanranalds out in the Jacobite cause. When the prince was on the run in South Uist the following year, however, Boisdale risked everything to help him, and the two spent a night of melancholy drunkenness in a remote hideout at Coradale shortly before Charles departed on his celebrated voyage to Skye.

Mollachdag

The story of the *Adelaar* lived on in island tradition, and in due course was recorded in print by the famous 'Coddy' – John MacPherson of Northbay (1876–1955):

> Once upon a time a ship was wrecked north of Ard Greian ... a Dutch ship she was, and there was a tremendous hurricane in the Atlantic and it was do or die for her and she made for the shore of Barra, and she could not make for a worse shore with the wind that was blowing and the sea that was running. And the ship became a total wreck on the reef of Mollachdag – that means in Gaelic 'the cursed rock' – unfortunately with the loss of all hands.

The identification of the reef to the north of Greian Head as Mollachdag – a name not to be found on any map – was confirmed in 1972 by John Maclean of Cliad, a croft adjacent to the

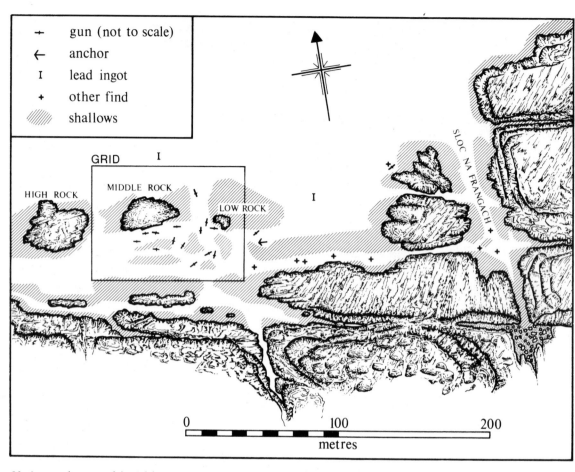

⊢	gun (not to scale)
←	anchor
I	lead ingot
+	other find
▨	shallows

GRID

HIGH ROCK

MIDDLE ROCK

LOW ROCK

SLOC NA FRANGACH

0   100   200

metres

83 A general survey of the *Adelaar* site.

84 Operating a metal detector over mobile pebbles filling a gully bottom. Note the vertical kelp-covered cliffs which rise to the surface.

site. An underwater search on 23 March by Chris Oldfield, Tony Long and Simon Martin easily located the *Adelaar*'s remains. They lay within and around a dramatic complex of deep gullies running through the reef and skirting its inshore edge. In places the gully sides are sheer, and plunge to a depth of 15 m (50 ft), although most of the wreckage lies in shallower water. The site is prone to extreme turbulence when the Atlantic swells break over the reef and is a hazardous and unpleasant place to dive. Later in 1972 a survey of the wreck was completed under the writer's direction, and limited excavation followed in 1974 (83, 84 and 85).

85 Excavating a narrow gully with a small dredge, powered
by a water-pump on the surface.

86 Some of the *Adelaar's* cargo of lead ingots, lying where they fell.

Contemporary accounts and the exposed location of the site both indicate that the break-up of the ship was almost instantaneous and extremely violent. Nevertheless, from an interpretation of the archaeological remains it is possible to reconstruct the sequence of events. The ship evidently first become wedged in the cleft between the middle and easternmost rocks, presumably during a desperate attempt to weather Greian Head at night. At this point her bottom ripped open, cascading heavy ballast – lead ingots and yellow Dutch building bricks – into the wide gully below (**86**).

The lightened hull then appears to have been lifted bodily by the exploding surf to smash down on the landward side of Mollachdag, where the main disintegration took place. This deposited many of the ship's guns and most of her heavier contents – including, it may be supposed, the treasure, still in the 17 locked chests bearing the seals of Captain de Keyser and Chief Merchant Troillaert – into the narrow gully which runs along the inshore edge of Mollachdag. Some sections of the broken vessel, however, were carried eastwards by the gale, taking one iron gun a distance of 200 metres (216 yds). Other material ended up in a deep inlet close to the shore, where silver coins and other objects have been found. Its name, *Sloch na Frangach* (Creek of the Foreigners), suggests that bodies came ashore here too.

No organic objects or parts of the hull have survived this dynamic environment, but heavier items – lead ingots and shot, iron cannon balls, tools and nails, articles of brass and copper, silver coins and a few pieces of gold jewellery – worked their way through the shingle to the gully bottoms and stabilized there. Most of this material was encased in concretion (**87**). In a few well-protected crevices fragments of yellow brick, a couple of clay pipes and some scraps of glass have survived the destructive abrasion which has destroyed most material of this kind.

The spread of iron and bronze guns at the core part of the site, which have probably not

87 Various iron objects recovered from concretion: left, nails and a staple; centre, hammer-heads and a hook; right, bar- and round-shot. Scale in cm.

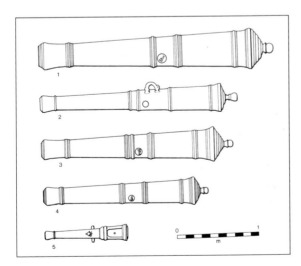

88 The five different types of gun carried by the *Adelaar*, as recorded from examples on the site.

moved far from the locations of their primary deposition, seems to reflect the original lie of the wreck, and closely matches the known dimensions of the ship.

Although both nature and the extensive salvage operations of 1728 have destroyed or removed most of the *Adelaar* and her contents, much can still be learned from a careful study of what remains. An investigation of the guns, for example, has provided a detailed snapshot of the actual weaponry carried by a VOC ship of this period (88). Though heavily concreted, the overall dimensions of the 14 cast-iron guns which remain on the site allow them to be classified according to the three types known to have been carried by the ship – 3-, 6-, and 12-pounders.

An example of each was chosen for de-concreting and recording in detail. The iron within, though much decomposed, still retained its original shape and surface detail. This

89 The 'F' mark (inverted) of the Swedish iron-foundry at Finspong on the trunnion-face of one of the *Adelaar's* guns. Scale in inches.

allowed features like mouldings and foundry marks to be identified. All the iron guns bore a letter 'F' on each trunnion face, indicating that they had been cast at the great Swedish foundry at Finspong, which supplied the Dutch East India Company with most of its cast-iron ordnance (89).

One 6-pounder, however, was of bronze, similar to a piece recovered by Captain Rowe in 1728. He had reported seeing the second one, but could not reach it because the gully in which it lay was too narrow to accommodate his bulky diving engine (90 and 91). These two bronze pieces were the guns adjacent to the compass, just as VOC regulations prescribed.

The eighteenth-century salvors also thoughtfully left behind a single example of the

eight bronze breech-loading swivel guns which the ship had carried. This one carries the VOC cipher on its barrel, although above it is the letter 'A' denoting that it was cast for the company's Amsterdam chamber rather than for the Middelburg one to which the *Adelaar* belonged (92). No doubt such equipment circulated freely within the company, regardless of where it originally came from.

In all, 38 ducatons, coins minted from Spanish American silver specifically for the East Indies trade, were recovered during the excavation. None of them were the fresh mintings of 1728 of which, it will be recalled, the *Adelaar's* consignment of 32,000 had been composed. This suggests that all the official coinage, probably still in its boxes, had been recovered by Mackenzie and Rowe. These examples, therefore, probably belonged to individuals aboard, perhaps for illegal trade on their own account (93).

90 One of the ship's two bronze 6-pounders, showing the effects of constant abrasion. The other was recovered in 1728.

91 Raising the bronze 6-pounder, which weighs nearly a ton, close to the exposed rocks of *Mollachdag* Sgeir. The ingenious lifting device was built by Chris Oldfield, here seen operating it.

92 The Dutch East India Company's A-VOC monogram on the breech of a bronze swivel gun.

93 Silver ducatons from the *Adelaar*: left, of the Dutch
United Provinces, with its republican emblem of a
mounted knight; right, of the Spanish Netherlands,
showing Philip IV. The United Provinces ducatons were
the staple of the East Indies trade, and were nicknamed
'silver riders'.

Three gold rings and a gold shirt-fastener
probably come from the bodies of victims who
perished in the wreck (**colour plate 13**). Other
personal objects are few and fragmentary: shoe
and belt buckles, a button, part of a pocket
watch, two clay pipes from Gouda, part of a
wine-glass stem, lead bird-shot and a fish hook.
Most of the other items recovered during the
excavation come from the ship's cargo of
hardware, and include different types of nails,
hammer-heads, copper bars, furniture fittings
and copper cooking utensils. Almost all can be
identified with the ship's inventories.

The *Adelaar* story ended, as it began, in a
court of law. Shortly after our team discovered
the wreck, a group of interlopers tried to muscle
in on the find, drawn by the lure of the treasure
which they believed still to be there. Protestations
that everything of monetary value had been
raised in 1728 evoked disbelief in our rivals, who
had seen the lead ingots lying scattered over the
seabed and thought they were bars of silver.

To preserve the archaeological integrity of the
wreck we took out an interdict against them, and
after due legal process the case was heard in
Edinburgh's Court of Session – successor to the
Admiralty Court in which the original case had
been heard in 1728. Happily, our case was less
protracted than its predecessor, for after seeing the
futility of pursuing the action further – by this time
it had become clear to everyone that the *Adelaar*
had no treasure to yield beyond archaeological
knowledge – the interlopers withdrew.

7
Scotland's sunken treasures

Six thousand years of seafaring

No one knows, and can probably never know, how many shipwrecks lie around our coasts. Even today, despite modern ship design, satellite navigation, safety regulations and emergency services, a tragically large number of vessels are wrecked each year in Scottish waters. In the mid nineteenth century, when detailed records began, the losses were even higher.

Though reliable figures for earlier periods do not exist, we can therefore be sure that floating craft have been wrecked ever since human beings first ventured out on our coastal waters.

How long ago that was no one can tell. But the mesolithic inhabitants of a seasonal hunting camp at Morton on the north-east coast of Fife, occupied sporadically between about 6000 and 4200 BC, were catching deep-sea fish, which must have required boats of some kind. Extensive mesolithic activity at Oban, and elsewhere in the Western Isles, suggests that water transport played a major part in the lives of these island hopping hunter-gatherer communities.

The craft they used were almost certainly dug-outs or skin boats (light frameworks covered with hides). Such boats have been used by traditional societies throughout the world since remote prehistory, and are still found in many places today. Dug-out craft (in their basic form no more than a hollowed-out log) are not well suited to the open sea, and were probably mainly confined to estuaries and inland waters.

Skin boats, on the other hand, can be wonderfully seaworthy vessels, as their still-functioning descendants, the tarred-canvas *curraghs* of Western Ireland, amply testify. There are several early historical references to such craft in Scottish waters, and it was in a skin-covered *curragh* that St Columba sailed from Ireland to Iona.

Many dug-outs have survived in Scotland, usually at the bottoms of lochs. They date from the prehistoric to the medieval periods. Skin boats are far less durable, though the 'ghost' of what may have been one has been recognized in a Bronze Age burial at Dalgety Bay, Fife. So far there is no indication as to whether complex wooden boats of the kind found at Dover and in the Humber Estuary were used in Bronze Age Scotland.

What sorts of vessels other than dug-outs and skin boats may have been used by the Iron Age peoples of Scotland, and their Dark Age successors, is not known. The few representations of boats in Pictish art give little clue as to how they were constructed. However, there was much Roman maritime activity in Scottish waters between the late first and early third centuries AD. The Roman governor Agricola, in his campaigns beyond the Forth in the early 80s, made extensive use of a fleet, which on at least one occasion appears to have circumnavigated Scotland. According to Tacitus, its vessels included *liburnians*, two-banked oared warships of Mediterranean type.

Agricola's troops may also have built vessels of a more local design, for the Roman army was always ready to adopt indigenous technologies. At Inchtuthil on the Tay, the site of a Roman legionary fortress established during the mid 80s, a specialized type of iron fastening associated with Celtic ship construction has been identified among the hoard of nails discovered there in the 1960s. River craft were probably used widely in Roman Scotland, and at the fort of Newstead on the bank of the Tweed a steering oar has been found.

During the mid second century the Antonine Wall appears to have been supported at either end by harbours in the Forth and Clyde, while it is clear that the massive armies which campaigned in Scotland under the emperor Septimius Severus in the early third century were provisioned almost entirely by sea.

Given the scale of this activity it is inconceivable that no Roman ships were wrecked in Scottish waters. None has yet been found, though the remains of several Spanish amphorae of second-century date found in a cave near Fife Ness are perhaps best explained as recoveries from a shipwreck on the nearby Carr Rocks.

The Scandinavian technique of building boats by creating 'shells' of overlapping planks, edge-jointed with iron rivets (the 'clinker' technique), was probably brought to Scotland by Viking raiders and settlers and has remained the traditional method of small-boat construction here ever since. As yet we know of no Viking wrecks, though ships were sometimes buried with their owners and these can be recognized by the surviving rows of iron fastenings even when all trace of the wooden planking has gone. A fine example was recently discovered at Scar in Orkney (**94**). That Viking wrecks may survive in our waters is hinted by the discovery of a Norse gold bracelet in the Sound of Mull, though this may perhaps be an isolated loss.

Traces of early Scottish clinker vessels occasionally turn up in the archaeological record. In the nineteenth century two roughed-out end pieces for a clinker boat of Viking type were discovered in a bog on the island of Eigg, where they had probably been buried for seasoning. Excavations in Perth High Street in the 1970s revealed, in a twelfth-century context, dismantled clinker boat components re-used as parts of domestic houses (**95**). The same site has produced numerous examples of the distinctive rivet-and-rove iron boat-fastenings, including unused strips of roves which suggest that boat building or repair had been practised in the vicinity (**96**). A clinker boat of probable medieval date was revealed in 1934 when Loch Laggan was partially drained for a hydroelectric scheme, though unfortunately it was neither preserved nor adequately recorded.

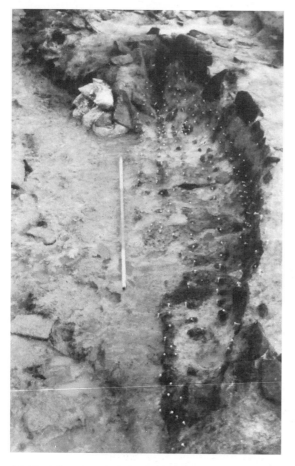

94 The Viking boat-burial at Scar, Orkney. The left side has been destroyed by coastal erosion; the right survives as an impression in the soil, its vanished planking traced out by lines of iron rivets.

95 An oak frame from a clinker-built boat from twelfth-century Perth, re-used in a timber house.

96 Unused roves from medieval Perth. Pieces from the strips could be broken off like chocolate.

So far no examples of the famous late medieval West Highland galleys have come to light, though they are well known from depictions on gravestones and the places from which they operated might still preserve, buried in the foreshores on which they were drawn up, remnants of these distinctive vessels (97). On the east coast of Scotland the medieval period saw the creation of coastal burghs and the opening up of trade with the Continent. Such records as we have show that ships and their cargoes were frequently lost, particularly in the approaches to the Forth and Tay, those great maritime highways into the heart of Scotland. A fourteenth-century Langerwehe jug dredged up by a trawler off the Isle of May probably comes from such a wreck (98). So too may the early fifteenth-century sword hilt and stone building blocks recovered from the Navity Bank, close to the entrance to the Dornoch Firth.

Scottish maritime activity intensified in the sixteenth and seventeenth centuries, with ships voyaging regularly to Norway, the Baltic,

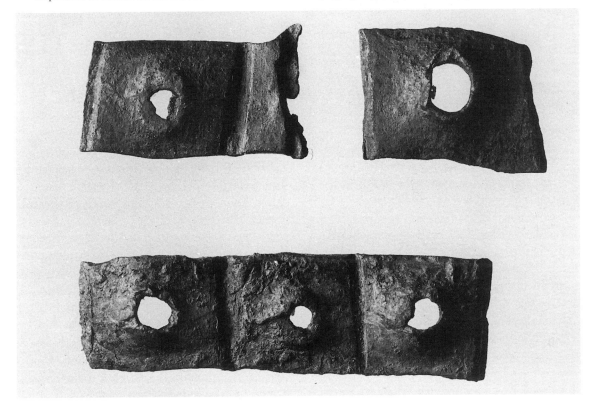

97 A late medieval Highland galley from a grave-slab
   on Iona.

Holland, France, Spain, and even North Africa.
Coastal trade within Britain itself was always
extensive. Later, from the west coast and
particularly Glasgow, Scottish shipping became
active in the transatlantic trade. Nor should we
forget the countless small vernacular craft which,
from the earliest times, have provided Scots men
and women with a ready means of
communication, local transportation and fishing.

   Much of the wreckage around our coast is of
relatively recent origin, but at least some of this
will be of archaeological relevance.
Paradoxically, such sites may be under greater

threat than those of the pre-industrial era, for
while wooden structures can survive almost
indefinitely in the right environments, iron and
steel are highly susceptible to corrosion in sea
water. Many early steamships sank in Scottish
waters. The remains of one of them, the
Irishman, which was built at Greenock in 1834
by John Scott (forerunner of the Scott-Lithgow
company), have been found off Skye, where she
was wrecked in 1862. The wreck of another
early Scottish steamship, the *Xantho*, built at
Dumbarton in 1848, has been located at Port
Gregory, Western Australia. This reminds us
that ships are highly mobile entities, and every
country's maritime archaeological resource has
an international dimension.

98 A fourteenth-century stoneware jug from Langerwehe (near Cologne), trawled up off the Isle of May at the entrance to the Forth. It probably comes from a medieval shipwreck.

An unbalanced record

In the light of the above it might seem surprising that the historic shipwrecks investigated in Scottish waters to date are so unrepresentative of the multifarious maritime activities which, for at least 6000 years, have been conducted around our shores. All are foreign, of post-medieval date, and either warships or large armed merchantmen belonging to powerful European trading interests. In addition to the six wrecks described in this book, remains of the following vessels have been discovered and investigated:

• **Unidentified wreck near Collieston, Aberdeenshire** This dispersed wreck lies in the vicinity of St Catherine's Dub, and local tradition associates the name with that of the ship, the *Santa Catalina*. Since 1840 a total of seven iron guns and an anchor have been recovered from the site, the most recent finds being made in 1970. The Armada origin which has been claimed for this wreck is unlikely, though the guns may be of late sixteenth-century date.

• **The *Lastdrager*, 1654** A Dutch East Indiaman lost near Cullivoe, Yell, in Shetland. Its much broken-up wreck was discovered and partially excavated by Robert Sténuit in 1971 and 1972. Recoveries included stoneware pottery, loose mercury, navigational and surgical instruments, coins, and various small finds. A Bellarmine flagon full of mercury found in a bog on the nearby island of Fetlar in 1881 probably came from this wreck.

• **The *Wrangels Palais*, 1687** A Danish warship wrecked off Bound Skerry in the Out Skerries, Shetland, not far from the *Kennemerland* site. Her remains were discovered in 1990 by Dr Tim Sharpe, a member of the team working on the *Kennemerland*. The site, which so far appears to consist mainly of a deposition of iron and bronze guns, has been extensively surveyed, and trial excavation carried out.

• *De Liefde*, 1711 Another broken-up and dispersed Dutch East Indiaman, found in 1964 off Mio Ness close to the southern tip of the Out Skerries. Several seasons of work by a number of teams have yielded many finds, including gold and silver coins, part of the ship's bell, pewter spoons, knife handles, a silver sword hilt, stoneware crucibles and other small objects. Some of this material is in the County Museum, Lerwick.

• **The *Curaçao*, 1729** A Dutch escort warship wrecked on Ship Stack, Unst. Her scattered remains, including five small bronze breech-loading swivel guns, were investigated by Robert Sténuit in 1972. Various small finds were recovered, including a fragment of a Dutch book on etiquette, preserved in concretion.

• The *Wendela*, 1737 A Danish East Indiaman lost on Fetlar in Shetland. This scattered site, found by Robert Sténuit in 1972, yielded a large number of silver coins. The range of national origins represented by the coins reflects the weakness of Danish currency at the time.

• The *Svecia*, 1740 A homeward-bound Swedish East Indiaman wrecked off North Ronaldsay in Orkney. Her much-dispersed remains were discovered in 1975 by Rex Cowan. Among the recoveries were quantities of dyewood from the ship's cargo.

• The *Drottningen af Swerige*, 1745 This Swedish East Indiaman (the name means *Queen of Sweden*) sank in Lerwick Harbour, Shetland. Her extensive remains were discovered in 1979 by Jean-Claude Joffre. Excavations have revealed a number of well-preserved finds, including ceramics, glass, pewterware, a gimballed brass lamp, a woodwind recorder, religious medallions and various objects of wood and leather.

• The *Evstafii*, 1780 A transport of the Imperial Russian Navy wrecked on Grif Skerry to the east of Whalsay in Shetland. Robert Sténuit found this scattered site in 1972, and recovered a considerable quantity of artefacts, including fragments of rope and sailcloth, weights, munitions (roundshot, bar shot, musket balls and grenades) and brass sword hilts. Among the wide assortment of small finds were brass pocket-sized icons and a silver medal commemorating the Russian naval victory at Tchesme in 1770.

Several factors explain this preponderance of post-medieval foreign wrecks. First, with the exception of the St Catherine's Dub wreck, the sites so far discovered by divers lie in exposed locations on the western seaboard of Scotland or among the Northern Isles. From the sixteenth century onwards these were hazardous sectors on a major European shipping route. Wrecks in such places often become extensively broken up and scattered, but significant parts of them remain unburied and therefore visible on the sea floor. This is particularly so in the case of large post-medieval armed vessels, whose massive cannons and anchors provide obvious and unmistakable markers of their presence. Finally, these exposed but largely silt-free littorals provide the best underwater visibility and diving conditions, so it is naturally here that most exploration has taken place.

Another factor has led to the discovery of these wrecks. In the course of the past four centuries shipping losses in this area have generated extensive documentation on the circumstances surrounding the disasters, and subsequent attempts at salvage. Much of this documentation survives today in archives, at home and abroad, and many of the sites we now know of were first located not on the sea floor but in the records of long-forgotten inquiries or lawsuits. Such occurrences also burned themselves deeply into local consciousness, often generating oral traditions which have continued into modern times.

For these reasons the wrecks which have been investigated by the first generation of underwater archaeologists in Scotland are not typical of the resource as a whole. Most of our historic shipwrecks, from the earliest times, probably lie along its eastern seaboard, particularly around the approaches to the Forth and Tay. But here the water is silty, and much of the sea floor is covered with deep sediments into which wrecks naturally penetrate, rendering them invisible but providing good conditions for preservation. These waters too, with their poor visibility and generally featureless seabeds, have not encouraged sport diving. We may presume therefore that the wrecks are there, and in abundance, although we do not know exactly where they lie or what they consist of.

But it is not too fanciful to suppose that remains from most of the ship and boat types which have ever sailed in Scottish waters will have survived within a variety of archaeological contexts, mainly but not exclusively underwater, and mostly along the east coast. This represents a precious but vulnerable heritage, for each site will be unique to its own particular time and purpose. No two will be quite alike, and the loss of any one will be irreplaceable.

For the most part this heritage is probably fairly secure, since the best- preserved sites are likely to be the ones which are invisibly buried in oxygen-free environments which ensure their almost indefinite survival. Unless such sites are threatened – as, for example, by undersea engineering work, fishing-gear impact or mineral extraction – there is little point at present even in seeking them, for the technologies and resources for properly excavating wrecks of this kind are simply not available. Their surest protection, for the moment at any rate, is for them to remain undiscovered.

A way forward

During the past 30 years the exposed and broken-up wreck sites of Scotland's Atlantic coasts and islands have provided a fruitful nursery for the development of underwater archaeology. Although some of the earlier ventures were aimed more at the recovery of valuables than of archaeological information, we have been spared the treasure-hunting depredations which have devastated shipwreck archaeology in other wreck-rich coastal areas. Since the early 1970s, moreover, Scotland has been at the forefront of academically-based underwater archaeology.

In 1973 St Andrews University established the Scottish Institute of Maritime Studies, which now has an international reputation and has conducted extensive underwater fieldwork on the *Gran Grifón*, *Swan*, *Dartmouth* and *Adelaar* sites. Other projects have been undertaken off Ireland. During the 1970s the late Keith Muckelroy, working first with the Institute and then with the National Maritime Museum at Greenwich, developed a methodology for studying wreck formation processes on which much further research has been based. The core of Muckelroy's investigation came from his long involvement with the *Kennemerland*, which has since become a type-site for the study of formation processes on scattered wrecks. These various projects, in addition to their own significance, have therefore been instrumental in establishing approaches and techniques relevant to the wider discipline.

St Andrews is also the home of the Archaeological Diving Unit (ADU), a government-sponsored team of diving archaeologists which visits wreck sites either designated under the Protection of Wrecks Act, or being considered for designation (see p. 119). Their remit covers the whole of the UK, and their job is to assess the significance of wreck sites, check their condition and ensure that work conducted by licensees is up to standard. The ADU acts as an important link between the sport-diving community and the archaeological establishment. Over the past ten years or so this has led to a growing spirit of co-operation between the two groups.

At the core of this constructive interaction is the Nautical Archaeology Society whose training programme, since 1983, has provided amateurs (diving and non-diving) with opportunities to learn nautical archaeological skills from an introductory level (the Part I qualification) to the near-professional standard of a Part IV. Scotland has an excellent base for these activities at the Lochaline Dive Centre in the Sound of Mull, though courses can be held at other locations by arrangement. Details are provided on p. 120.

Since it took responsibility for designating and administering historic shipwreck sites in 1992, Historic Scotland has been active in this new area of heritage resource management. Uniquely in the UK, it assesses historic shipwrecks using the same criteria which it applies to archaeological sites on land, and has provided funding for underwater rescue work, particularly on the *Swan* site at Duart Point. In addition to excavation, this has allowed long-term programmes of site stabilization and *in situ* conservation to be initiated (**colour plates 14 and 15**).

99 Archaeologically-trained amateur divers, working closely with archaeologists who dive, are keys to the effective stewardship of Scotland's rich underwater heritage.

Another Historic Scotland innovation is the establishment, first on the *Swan* site and later on the *Dartmouth*, of a scheme whereby amateur divers can visit these protected wrecks on open days and follow labelled trails around them (**colour plate 16**). Information boards for terrestrial visitors are now being erected on the shore adjacent to historic wreck sites (**colour plate 17**).

Scottish museums have played an important role in conserving and curating recoveries from wrecks. The Shetland County Museum has a rich collection on display, including recoveries from the *Gran Grifón* and *Kennemerland* sites, while

the National Museums of Scotland are currently conserving the extensive groups of material from the *Dartmouth* and *Swan*. Much of this work involves the difficult and expensive business of dealing with waterlogged organic artefacts, and this has generated new research at St Andrews University into a process for conserving organic materials using supercritical drying.

Information about shipwrecks and other archaeological sites below High Water Mark is gathered by the National Monuments Record of Scotland, and a computerized database is available for maritime researchers. This is a two-way process, and divers and other fieldworkers are encouraged to send information to the address given on p. 120 for inclusion in the database.

All these developments bode well for the next generation of underwater archaeologists in

Scotland. The priority should be to expand our knowledge of the more exposed wrecks on the northern and western seaboards so that these sites can be assessed, monitored, and protected if necessary. At the same time a watching brief over the east coast should be maintained, and areas of seabed scheduled for development assessed for any archaeological content. Nor should the more exposed areas of the eastern seaboard, particularly around the approaches to harbours, be ignored.

If the necessary professional support was available much of this work could be done by amateur divers with a basic training in archaeology (**99**). There are perhaps 100,000 active sport divers in Britain, and many are either based in Scotland or come here on holiday. Groups might adopt their local 'patches' and, with guidance, would be well-placed both to explore and monitor specific parts of the coastline. Many would probably be keen to do so, and all that is needed to make such a scheme effective is an infrastructure to pull it together. Most of the necessary components are already in place.

Only in exceptional cases where, as at Duart, a site is under environmental or other threat, should direct archaeological intervention be considered. Such work will require the availability of a small cadre of professional diving archaeologists, who will also be needed to support and co-ordinate the amateur effort. Some of these individuals may come from within the amateur groups, as they acquire for themselves a growing level of skill and experience.

Others may be trained archaeologists who have learned to dive, for the underwater environment will be archaeology's great challenge in the new millennium. Shipwrecks are only part of our underwater heritage. The scope of this book has not allowed a consideration of submerged habitation sites, like the prehistoric crannogs and sunken duns investigated by Dr Nicholas Dixon of Edinburgh University, which provide ideal environments for rich deposits of organic archaeological material and environmental evidence. Scotland abounds in such sites, and many of our future archaeologists will have to be divers as well.

Appendix

Underwater archaeology and the law

The laws concerning recoveries from the seabed, especially when these are of an archaeological nature, are complex, and it is not within the scope of this book to set them out in detail. But responsible divers and other users of the sea will find the various agencies that they have to deal with constructive and helpful. Anyone involved in such activities should seek appropriate advice.

The Protection of Wrecks Act, 1973

The Secretary of State for Scotland is empowered to designate shipwrecks of historic significance. Designation prohibits diving on or otherwise interfering with the site concerned except under licence. At the time of writing the following wrecks in Scottish territorial waters are designated:

Swan, 1653 (Duart Point, Mull)
Kennemerland, 1664 (Out Skerries, Shetland)
Wrangels Palais, 1687 (Out Skerries, Shetland)
Dartmouth, 1690 (Eilean Rubha an Ridire, Sound of Mull)

New designations are promulgated through Notices to Mariners and other media. It is the responsibility of individuals to ensure that they do not infringe designation orders.

The Protection of Military Remains Act, 1986

This Act provides for the protection of specified vessels sunk or stranded while in military service after 4 August 1914; UK vessels may be protected in international waters, while in UK waters vessels of any nationality may be protected. An area within UK waters containing a vessel sunk within the last 200 years may also be designated.

For further information and advice contact:

Historic Scotland
Longmore House
Salisbury Place
Edinburgh EH9 1SH
Tel: 0131 668 8765
Fax: 0131 668 8788

The Archaeological Diving Unit
University of St Andrews
Fife KY16 9AJ
Tel: 01334 462919
Fax: 01334 462921

The Receiver of Wreck

All recoveries from below High Water Mark, irrespective of their age or ownership, must be reported to:

The Receiver of Wreck
Spring Place
105 Commercial Road
Southampton SO151EG
Tel: 01703 329474
Fax: 01703 329477

Nautical Archaeology Society

Information about Protected Shipwreck visitor trails, and the Nautical Archaeology Society's training programme, can be obtained from:

The NAS Training Officer (Scotland)
c/o Lochaline Dive Centre
Lochaline
Morvern
Argyll PA34 5XT
Tel/Fax: 01967 421627

For further information about the Society and its activities, including membership, contact:

Nautical Archaeology Society
c/o 19 College Road
HM Naval Base
Portsmouth PO1 3LJ
Tel/Fax: 01705 818419

Royal Commission on the Ancient and Historic Monuments of Scotland

For information about the maritime database contact:

National Monuments Record of Scotland
RCAHM Scotland
John Sinclair House
16 Bernard Terrace
Edinburgh EH8 9NX
Tel: 0131 662 1456
Fax: 0131 662 1477 or *0131 662 1499*

Glossary

Note: some of these terms may have several meanings depending on the contexts in which they are used. They are defined here according to usage in this book.

argosy A big merchant vessel from Ragusa (Dubrovnik).

arquebusier A Spanish soldier armed with the **arquebus**, a light firearm. The Scottish equivalent (p. 00) was 'hagbutter'.

backstaff A navigational instrument for measuring the sun's altitude.

ballast Additional weight carried in a ship's hold to provide stability.

binnacle Wooden housing for a ship's compasses.

birlin A Highland galley, often used for war.

caper A small pirate vessel.

clinker A form of hull construction using overlapping planks joined at their edges.

con To guide or steer a ship.

corsair A **privateer**, especially one from Islamic parts of the Mediterranean.

deadeye A circular block with three holes, used for tightening rigging.

fire-ship A vessel filled with combustibles and explosives, set alight and allowed to drift towards an enemy.

fly-boat A shallow-draught inshore craft.

frigate A medium-sized fast warship, usually a 5th **rate**.

gabion Basketwork tube filled with earth to make defensive works.

galleon A long sailing warship with low castleworks fore and aft.

hulk A tubby cargo vessel from the Baltic.

limber An articulated pair of wheels, hitched to the trail of a gun-carriage so that it could be towed by draught animals.

morion A distinctive type of brimmed and crested helmet.

musketeer A soldier armed with a heavy **musket**, which was generally fired from a forked rest.

pinnace A term frequently applied to a ship's boat, but also used to describe a light and fast fighting ship of Dutch design, often used for piracy.

privateer A privately-owned vessel authorized by its government to prey on enemy shipping.

quintal A Spanish weight measurement of 100 Castilian pounds.

rate The size of a British warship, defined by her captain's rate of pay. The rates ran from 1st (the largest) to 6th.

rivet and rove The headed fastening and its fixing washer used to join the **strakes** of a **clinker** boat.

rudder pintle One of the pins, usually of iron, by which the rudder was hung on a ship's **stern-post**.

scupper-liner A lead pipe running through the side of a ship to drain water from the deck.

sheave A pulley-wheel.

sloop A small warship.

snaphaunce A firing mechanism for muskets and pistols, precursor of the flintlock.

stem-post The forward upright member of a ship's structure, extending upwards from the keel. The **stern-post** was the corresponding member aft.

strake A complete run of planking along a ship's hull.

trenail (*lit.* 'tree-nail') A wooden peg, usually of oak, used to fasten the planks of a ship's hull.

trunnions The paired cylindrical pivots by which a gun was elevated on its carriage. Trunnions on iron guns frequently bear a manufacturer's mark.

Further reading

Note: *The International Journal of Nautical Archaeology* is abbreviated *IJNA*.

General

Martin Dean, Ben Ferrari, Ian Oxley, Mark Redknap and Kit Watson (eds), *Archaeology Underwater: the NAS Guide to Principles and Practice*, second edition, London, 1995.

Colin Martin and Geoffrey Parker, *The Spanish Armada*, London, 1988.

The wrecks

Entries appear in the order of wreck sites discussed, not in alphabetical order.

Alison McLeay, *The Tobermory Treasure*, London, 1986.

Colin Martin, *Full Fathom Five: the wrecks of the Spanish Armada*, London, 1975.

Colin Martin, '*El Gran Grifón*: an Armada wreck off Fair Isle', *IJNA* 1 (1972), 59–71.

Colin Martin, 'A Cromwellian shipwreck off Duart Point, Mull: an interim report', *IJNA* (1995) **24**, 1: 15–32.

John R. Adnams, 'The *Dartmouth*, a British frigate wrecked off Mull, 1690', *IJNA* (1974) **3**, 2: 269–74.

Roger G. Holman, 'The *Dartmouth*, a British frigate wrecked off Mull, 1690. 2. Culinary and related items', *IJNA* (1975) **4**, 2: 253–65.

Peter McBride, 'The *Dartmouth*, a British frigate wrecked off Mull, 1690. 3. The guns', *IJNA* (1976) **5**, 3: 189–200.

Paula Martin, 'The *Dartmouth*, a British frigate wrecked off Mull, 1690. 4. The clay pipes', *IJNA* (1977) **6**, 3: 219–23.

Colin Martin, 'The *Dartmouth*, a British frigate wrecked off Mull, 1690. 5. The ship', *IJNA* (1978) **7**, 1: 29–58.

W.A. Foster and K.B. Higgs, 'The *Kennemerland*, 1971: an interim report', *IJNA* (1973) **2**, 2: 291–300.

Richard Price and Keith Muckelroy, 'The second season of work on the *Kennemerland* site, 1973', *IJNA* (1974) **3**, 2: 257–68.

Richard Price and Keith Muckelroy, 'The *Kennemerland* site. The third and fourth seasons 1974 & 1976', *IJNA* (1977) **6**, 3: 187–218.

Richard Price and Keith Muckelroy, 'The *Kennemerland* site, the fifth season, 1978', *IJNA* (1979) **8**, 4: 311–20.

Richard Price, Keith Muckelroy and Lynn Willes, 'The *Kennemerland* site, a report on the lead ingots', *IJNA* (1980) **9**, 1: 7–25.

Christopher Dobbs and Richard Price, 'The *Kennemerland* site. The sixth and seventh seasons, 1984 & 1987, and the identification of five golf clubs', *IJNA* (1991) **20**, 2: 111–22

Colin Martin, 'The wreck of the Dutch East Indiaman *Adelaar* off Barra in 1728', *in* Roger Mason and Norman Macdougall (eds), *People and Power in Scotland; essays in honour of T.C. Smout,* Edinburgh, 1992: 145–69.

Robert Sténuit, 'Early relics of the VOC trade from Shetland: the wreck of the flute *Lastdrager* lost off Yell, 1653', *IJNA* (1974) **3**, 2: 213–56.

Mensun Bound and Tim Sharpe, 'The wreck of the Danish man-of-war *Wrangels Palais* (1687) off Bound Skerry in the Out Skerries (Shetland Islands)' *in* Mensun Bound (ed.), *The Archaeology of Ships of War*, Oswestry, 1995: 45–51.

Alan Bax and Colin Martin, '*De Liefde*: a Dutch East Indiaman lost on the Out Skerries, Shetland, in 1711', *IJNA* (1974) **3**, 1: 81–90.

Robert Sténuit, 'The wreck of the *Curaçao*: a Dutch warship lost off Shetland in 1729', *IJNA* (1977) **6**, 2: 101–25.

Louise Joffre, 'The *Queen of Sweden* – three years later', *Scottish Diver*, September–October 1985.

Robert Sténuit, 'The wreck of the pink *Evstafii*: A transport of the Imperial Russian Navy lost off Shetland in 1780', *IJNA* (1976) **5**, 3: 221–43.

Index

All names of ships are in *italics*

(Page numbers in **bold** refer to illustrations)

The author

Dr Colin Martin is a Reader in Maritime Studies at the University of St Andrews. During the past thirty years he has carried out excavations on several historic shipwrecks in Scottish and Irish waters. He is currently investigating a Cromwellian wreck off Mull in association with Historic Scotland and the National Museum of Scotland.

Series editor: Dr David J. Breeze
Chief Inspector of Ancient Monuments,
Historic Scotland